SPANISH SENTENCE BUILDERS

A lexicogrammar approach

Beginner to Pre-Intermediate

SECOND EDITION

Imprint: Independently Published
Edited by Verónica Palacín

About the authors

Gianfranco Conti taught for 25 years at schools in Italy, the UK and in Kuala Lumpur, Malaysia. He has also been a university lecturer, holds a Master's degree in Applied Linguistics and a PhD in metacognitive strategies as applied to second language writing. He is now an author, a popular independent educational consultant and professional development provider. He has written around 2,000 resources for the TES website, which have awarded him the Best Resources Contributor in 2015. He has co-authored the best-selling and influential book for world languages teachers, "The Language Teacher Toolkit" and "Breaking the sound barrier: Teaching learners how to listen", in which he puts forth his Listening As Modelling methodology. Gianfranco writes an influential blog on second language acquisition called The Language Gym, co-founded the interactive website language-gym.com and the Facebook professional group Global Innovative Language Teachers (GILT). Last but not least, Gianfranco has created the instructional approach known as E.P.I. (Extensive Processing Instruction).

Dylan Viñales has taught for 15 years, in schools in Bath, Beijing and Kuala Lumpur in state, independent and international settings. He lives in Kuala Lumpur. He is fluent in five languages, and gets by in several more. Dylan is, besides a teacher, a professional development provider, specialising in E.P.I., metacognition, teaching languages through music (especially ukulele) and cognitive science. In the last five years, together with Dr Conti, he has driven the implementation of E.P.I. in one of the top international schools in the world: Garden International School. This has allowed him to test, on a daily basis, the sequences and activities included in this book with excellent results (his students have won language competitions both locally and internationally). He has designed an original Spanish curriculum, bespoke instructional materials, based on Reading and Listening as Modelling (RAM and LAM). Dylan co-founded the fastest growing professional development group for modern languages teachers on Facebook, Global Innovative Languages Teachers, which includes over 12,000 teachers from all corners of the globe. He authors an influential blog on modern language pedagogy in which he supports the teaching of languages through E.P.I. Dylan is the lead author of Spanish content on the Language Gym website and oversees the technological development of the site. He is currently undertaking the NPQML qualification, after which he plans to pursue a Masters in second language acquisition.

Acknowledgements

Writing a book is a time-consuming yet rewarding endeavour. Dylan would like to thank his wife, Natasha, for her help and support, for being an amazing mother and partner; and for not telling the kids where he was hiding while he wrote his part of the book. He would also like to thank his parents, John and Angie, for their unconditional and unwavering support and love.

Secondly, a huge thanks to our editor, Verónica Palacín, from Barbastro, Huesca, Spain. She is always a pleasure to work with; good humoured, extremely dedicated and with an eagle-eye. Her contributions have gone **far** beyond proofreading for accuracy, into advising on best selection of language content, and offering inter-cultural boosts along the way. She has been a real asset to our team.

Thirdly, heartfelt thanks to Tom Ball, Damian Graizevsky and David James, at Garden International School, for being fantastic colleagues, inspiring leaders, and for helping to create a world class working environment, where it was possible to lay the foundations for E.P.I. and produce the bank of Sentence Builders that are the foundation for this booklet.

In addition, a shout-out to the talented Ross Padgett, former Head of Art at Garden International School for his superb work designing the book cover.

Thank you to our trusted friends and colleagues Tom Ball (again), Alfonso Maldonado and Roberto Jover Soro, for their invaluable help in "ironing out the rough spots" by helping with the final round of proofreading.

In addition, Dylan would like to thank his eagle-eyed students Igyeom Park, Tim He, Rivan Jain, Tiam Lak, Manvita Bharath & Aahana Singh for their ongoing efforts to proofread and help fine-tune this book.

A special mention to the ever-dedicated and generous Joe Evans, for his time and moral support during the final review of the first edition.

Lastly, many thanks to the talented & methodical Inés Glowacka for her contributions to the extra proofreading of the second - more accurate than ever before - edition. Your time, expertise and energy is greatly appreciated!

Gracias a todos.

Introduction

Hello and welcome to the first 'text' book designed to be an accompaniment to a Spanish, Extensive Processing Instruction course. The book has come about out of necessity, because such a resource did not previously exist.

How to use this book if you have bought into our E.P.I. approach

This book was originally designed as a resource to use in conjunction with our E.P.I. approach and teaching strategies. Our course favours flooding comprehensible input, organising content by communicative functions and related constructions, and a big focus on reading and listening as modelling. The aim of this book is to empower the beginner-to-pre-intermediate learner with linguistic tools - high-frequency structures and vocabulary - useful for real-life communication. Since, in a typical E.P.I. unit of work, aural and oral work play a huge role, this book should not be viewed as the ultimate E.P.I. coursebook, but rather as a **useful resource** to **complement** your Listening-As-Modelling and Speaking activities.

Sentence Builders – Online Versions

Please note that all these sentence builders will be available in bilingual and Spanish only versions on the Language Gym website, available to download, editable and optimised for displaying in the classroom, via the Locker Room section (available via subscription).

How to use this book if you don't know or have NOT bought into our approach

Alternatively, you may use this book to dip in and out of as a source of printable material for your lessons. Whilst our curriculum is driven by communicative functions rather than topics, we have deliberately embedded the target constructions in topics which are popular with teachers and commonly found in published coursebooks.

If you would like to learn about E.P.I. you could read one of the authors' blogs. The definitive guide is Dr Conti's "Patterns First – How I Teach Lexicogrammar" which can be found on his blog (www.gianfrancoconti.com). There are also blogs on Dylan's wordpress site (mrvinalesmfl.wordpress.com) such as "Using sentence builders to reduce (everyone's) workload and create more fluent linguists" which can be read to get teaching ideas and to learn how to structure a course, through all the stages of E.P.I.

The book "Breaking the Sound Barrier: Teaching Learners how to Listen" by Gianfranco Conti and Steve Smith, provides a detailed description of the approach and of the listening and speaking activities you can use in synergy with the present book.

The basic structure of the book

The book contains 19 macro-units which concern themselves with a specific communicative function, such as 'Describing people's appearance and personality', 'Comparing and contrasting people', 'Saying what you like and dislike' or 'Saying what you and others do in your free time'. You can find a note of each communicative function in the Table of Contents. Each unit includes:

- a sentence builder modelling the target constructions;
- a set of vocabulary building activities which reinforce the material in the sentence builder;
- a set of narrow reading texts exploited through a range of tasks focusing on both the meaning and structural levels of the text;
- a set of translation tasks aimed at consolidation through retrieval practice;
- a set of writing tasks targeting essential writing micro-skills such as spelling, functional and positional processing, editing and communication of meaning.

Each sentence builder at the beginning of a unit contains one or more constuctions which have been selected with real-life communication in mind. Each unit is built around that construction <u>but not solely on it</u>. Based on the principle that each E.P.I instructional sequence must move from modelling to production in a seamless and organic way, each unit expands on the material in each sentence builder by embedding it in texts and graded tasks which contain both familiar and unfamiliar (but comprehensible and learnable) vocabulary and structures. Through lots of careful recycling and thorough and extensive processing of the input, by the end of each unit the student has many opportunities to encounter and process the new vocabulary and patterns with material from the previous units.

Alongside the macro-units you will find:

- grammar units: one or two pages of activities occurring at regular intervals. They explicitly focus on key grammar structures which enhance the generative power of the constructions in the sentence builders. At this level they mainly concern themselves with full conjugations of key verbs, with agreement and preposition usage. Note that these units recycle the same verbs many times over by revisiting at regular intervals but in different linguistic contexts;
- question-skills units: one or two pages on understanding and creating questions. These micro-units too occur at regular intervals in the book, so as to recycle the same question patterns in different linguistic contexts;
- revision quickies: these are retrieval practice tasks aimed at keeping the previously learnt vocabulary alive. These too occur at regular intervals;
- self-tests: these occur at the end of the book. They are divided into two sections, one for less confident and one for more confident learners.

The point of all the above micro-units is to implement lots of systematic recycling and interleaving, two techniques that allow for stronger retention and transfer of learning.

 **THE LANGUAGE GYM**

Important *caveat*

1) This is a '**no frills**' book. This means that there are a limited number of illustrations (only on unit title pages). This is because we want every single little thing in this book to be useful. Consequently, we have packed a substantive amount of content at the detriment of its outlook. In particular, we have given serious thought to both **recycling** and **interleaving**, in order to allow for key constructions, words and grammar items to be revisited regularly so as to enhance exponentially their retention.

2) **Listening** as modelling is an essential part of E.P.I. There will be an accompanying listening booklet released shortly which will contain narrow listening exercises for all 19 units, following the same content as this book.

3) **All content** in this booklet matches the content on the **Language Gym** website. For best results, we recommend a mixture of communicative, retrieval practice games, combined with Language Gym games and workouts, and then this booklet as the follow-up, either in class or for homework.

4) An **answer booklet** is also available, for those that would like it. We have produced it separately to stop this booklet from being excessively long.

5) This booklet is suitable for **beginner** to **pre-intermediate** learners. This equates to a **CEFR A1-A2** level, or a beginner **Y6-Y8** class. You do not need to start at the beginning, although you may want to dip in to certain units for revision/recycling. You do not need to follow the booklet in order, although many of you will, and if you do, you will benefit from the specific recycling/interleaving strategies. Either way, all topics are repeated frequently throughout the book.

We do hope that you and your students will find this book useful and enjoyable.

Gianfranco and Dylan

TABLE OF CONTENTS

 **THE LANGUAGE GYM**

THE LANGUAGE GYM

UNIT 1
Talking about my age

In this unit you will learn:

- How to say your name and age
- How to say someone else's name and age
- How to count from 1 to 16
- A range of common Spanish names
- The words for brother and sister

Tengo un año

Tengo diez años

Tengo seis años

Tengo quince años

THE LANGUAGE GYM

1

UNIT 1
Talking about my age

Me llamo *I am called*				tengo *I have**	un	1	año *year*
Mi hermano *My brother* **Mi hermana** *My sister*	**se llama** *is called*	Alejandro Antonio Arantxa Belén Carlos Diego Emilia Felipe Isabel José Julián María Paco Roberto	**y** *and*	**tiene** *he/she has**	dos tres cuatro cinco seis siete ocho nueve diez once doce trece catorce quince dieciséis	2 3 4 5 6 7 8 9 10 11 12 13 14 15 16	años *years*

Author's notes:

1) The number "uno" becomes "un" when it goes before a noun.

e.g. "Tengo un hermano".

2) In Spanish, we use the verb "to have" for age. So, we say "tengo diez años" to say how old we are, even though it means, literally "I have ten years". There are a few Latin languages (e.g. Italian/French) that do this :D

Unit 1. Talking about my age: VOCABULARY BUILDING

1. Match up

un año	seven years
dos años	four years
tres años	five years
cuatro años	six years
cinco años	eleven years
seis años	ten years
siete años	twelve years
ocho años	nine years
nueve años	two years
diez años	eight years
once años	one year
doce años	three years

2. Complete with the missing word

a. Tengo _catorce_ años   *I am fourteen years old*

b. Mi hermano _se_ llama Felipe   *My brother is called Felipe*

c. Me _llamo_ Diego   *My name is Diego*

d. Mi hermano _tiene_ dos años   *My brother is two*

e. Mi hermana tiene _cuatro_ años   *My sister is four*

f. _me_ llamo Ana   *My name is Ana*

cuatro	tiene	se
me	catorce	llamo

3. Translate into English

a. Tengo tres años

b. Tengo cinco años

c. Tengo once años

d. Tiene quince años

e. Tiene trece años

f. Tiene siete años

g. Mi hermano

h. Mi hermana

i. Se llama

4. Broken words

a. Ten_____ *I have*

b. Me lla____ *my name is*

c. Mi herm_____ *my sister*

d. Qui_____ *fifteen*

e. Dieci_____ *sixteen*

f. On_____ *eleven*

g. Nu_____ *nine*

h. Cato_____ *fourteen*

i. Do_____ *twelve*

5. Rank the people below from oldest to youngest as shown in the example

Miguel tiene quince años	1
María tiene trece años	2
Francisco tiene dos años	7
Pablo tiene cuatro años	5
Alejandro tiene un año	8
Roberta tiene cinco años	4
Arantxa tiene nueve años	3
Marta tiene tres años	6

6. For each pair of people write who is the oldest, as shown in the example

A	B	OLDER
Tengo once años	Tengo trece años	B
Tengo tres años	Tengo seis años	B
Tengo once años	Tengo doce años	B
Tengo quince años	Tengo trece años	A
Tengo catorce años	Tengo once años	A
Tengo ocho años	Tengo nueve años	B
Tengo once años	Tengo siete años	A

Unit 1. Talking about my age: READING

Me llamo Nico. Soy argentino. Tengo doce años y vivo en Buenos Aires, la capital de Argentina. Tengo un hermano que se llama Antonio. Antonio tiene catorce años.

Me llamo Ramón. Soy español. Tengo diez años y vivo en Madrid, la capital de España. Tengo una hermana que se llama Bárbara y un hermano que se llama Paco. Bárbara tiene cinco años. Paco tiene nueve años.

Me llamo Marco. Soy italiano. Tengo trece años y vivo en Roma, la capital de Italia. Tengo un hermano que se llama Robbie. Robbie tiene quince años.

Me llamo Marine. Soy francesa. Tengo diez años y vivo en París, la capital de Francia. Tengo una hermana que se llama Fabienne. Fabienne tiene once años. También tengo un hermano que se llama Pierre. Pierre tiene ocho años.

1. Find the Spanish for the following items in Nico's text

a. I am Argentinian
Soy argentino

b. I am called
me llamo

c. the capital
la capital

d. in Buenos Aires
en Buenos Aires

e. who is called Antonio
se llama Antonio

f. I am twelve
tengo doce años

g. is fourteen
Catorce años

2. Answer the following questions about Ramón

a. Where is Ramón from?
Madrid. Spain

b. How old is he?
10 years old

c. How many siblings does he have?
two

d. What are their names and ages?
Barbra - 5
Paco - 9

Me llamo Kaori. Soy japonesa. Tengo siete años y vivo en Tokyo, la capital de Japón. Tengo una hermana que se llama Yoko. Yoko tiene trece años. También tengo un hermano que se llama Hiroto. Hiroto tiene diez años.

3. Complete the table below

	Age	Nationality	How many siblings	Ages of siblings
Marco	13	italian	1	15
Nico	12	argentinian	1	14
Ramón	10	spanish	2	5, 9

Me llamo Hans. Soy alemán. Tengo catorce años y vivo en Berlín, en Alemania. Tengo dos hermanos. Mi hermano mayor se llama Patrick y mi hermano menor se llama Philip. Patrick tiene dieciséis años y Philip tiene quince años.

4. Hans, Kaori or Marine?

a. Who is from Germany? - *Hans*

b. Who has an 11-year-old sister? - *Marine*

c. Who is 11? -

d. Who has an older brother aged 16? - *Hans*

e. Who has a 15-year old brother? - *Hans*

THE LANGUAGE GYM

Unit 1. Talking about my age: TRANSLATION

1. Faulty translation: spot and correct (in the English) any translation mistakes you find below

a. Me llamo Patricia: _Her name is Patricia_
my name

b. Tengo dos hermanas: _I have two brothers_
sisters

c. Mi hermana se llama Marta: _My mother is called Marta_
sister

d. Mi hermano tiene cinco años: _My sister is 5_
brother

e. Tengo quince años: _I am five_
15

f. Mi hermano tiene ocho años: _My brother is seven_
eight

g. No tengo hermanos: _I don't have a sister_
siblings

h. Tengo dieciséis años: _I am 17_
16

i. Tengo doce años: _I am 13_
12

j. Se llama Juan: _My name is Juan_
his name

2. From Spanish to English

a. Mi hermano se llama Juan.
my brothers name is Juan

b. Tengo quince años.
i am 15

c. Mi hermano tiene seis.
my brother is 6

d. Mi hermana se llama Mariana.
my sister is called Mariana

e. Tengo siete años.
i am 7

f. Vivo en Madrid.
i live in madrid

g. Mi hermana tiene catorce años.
my sister is 14

h. Tengo un hermano y una hermana.
I have a brother and sister

i. María tiene doce años.
Maria is 12

j. Arantxa tiene nueve años.
Arantxa is 9

3. English to Spanish translation

a. My name is Paco. I am six.
me llamo Paco. Tengo seis años

b. My brother is fifteen years old.
mi hermano es quince años

c. I am twelve.
Tengo doce años

d. My sister is called Arantxa.
Mi hermana se llama Arantxa

e. I am fourteen.
Tengo catorce años

f. I have a brother and a sister.
Tengo un hermano y una hermana

g. My name is Felipe and I am fourteen.
me llamo Felipe y tengo catorce años

h. My name is Gabriel and I am eleven.
me llamo gabriel y tengo once años

i. My name is Santiago. I am ten. I have a brother and a sister.
me llamo Santiago. Tengo diez. Tengo un hermano y una hermana

j. My sister is called Ana. She is twelve.
mi hermana se llama Ana. Tiene doce años

THE LANGUAGE GYM

Unit 1. Talking about my age: WRITING

1. Complete the words

a. M_e_ ll_amo_ Paco

b. Te_ngo_ cato_rce_ a_ños_

c. _Te_ngo un_a_ h_ermana_a

d. M_i_ h_erman_o se ll_ama_ Julio

e. Me _lla_mo Patricio

f. Mi _he_rmano s_e_ _lla_ma Pablo

g. _Tengo_ tr_ec_e años

h. Mi he_rman_a se ll_ama_ Ana

2. Write out the numbers in Spanish

nine — n_ueve_

seven — s_iete_

twelve — d_oce_

five — c_inco_

fourteen — c_atorce_

sixteen — d_ieciseis_

thirteen — t_rece_

four — c_uatro_

3. Spot and correct the spelling mistakes

a. Me lamo Paco.
llamo

b. Tengo trece anos.
años

c. Mi hermano tene cinco anos.
tiene

d. Mi hermano se llama María.
hermana

e. Mi llamo Patricio.
me

f. Mi hermana se llamo Alejandra.
hermano

4. Complete with a suitable word

a. Mi hermana se _____ Laura.

b. _____ hermano tiene quince años.

c. Me _____ Mario.

d. Tengo un _____ que se llama Felipe.

e. Tengo una _____ que se llama Arantxa.

f. Mi hermano _____ catorce años.

5. Guided writing – write 4 short paragraphs in the first person singular 'I' each describing the people below

	Age	Lives in	Nationality	Brother's name and age	Sister's name and age
Samuel	12	Buenos Aires	Argentinian	Gonzalo 9	Anna 8
Rebeca	15	Madrid	Spanish	Jaime 13	Valentina 5
Michael	11	Berlin	German	Thomas 7	Gerda 12
Kyoko	10	Osaka	Japanese	Ken 6	Rena 1

6. Describe this person in the third person:

Name: Jorge

Age: 12

Lives in: Barcelona

Brother: Mario, 13 years old

Sister: Soledad, 15 years old

 **THE LANGUAGE GYM**

UNIT 2
Saying when my birthday is

In this unit you will learn to say:

- Where you and another person (e.g. a friend) are from
- When your birthday is
- Numbers from 15 to 31
- Months
- I am / He is / She is
- Names of Spanish speaking locations
- Where you live

UNIT 2
Saying when my birthday is

Me llamo José *My name is José*	**soy de Madrid** *I am from Madrid* ***tengo X años** *I am X years old*	**y** *and* **mi cumpleaños es el** *my birthday is the*	1 - uno / primero 2 - dos 3 - tres 4 - cuatro 5 - cinco 6 - seis 7 - siete 8 - ocho 9 - nueve 10 - diez 11 - once 12 - doce 13 - trece 14 - catorce 15 - quince 16 - dieciséis 17 - diecisiete 18 - dieciocho 19 - diecinueve 20 - veinte 21 - veintiuno 22 - veintidós 23 - veintitrés 24 - veinticuatro 25 - veinticinco 26 - veintiséis 27 - veintisiete 28 - veintiocho 29 - veintinueve 30 - treinta 31 - treinta y uno	**de** *of*	**enero** *January* **febrero** **marzo** **abril** **mayo** **junio** **julio** **agosto** **septiembre** **octubre** **noviembre** **diciembre**
Mi amiga se llama Catalina *My friend is called Catalina* **Mi amigo se llama Francisco** *My friend is called Francisco*	**es de Bilbao** *he/she is from Bilbao* ***tiene X años** *he/she is X years old*	**y** *and* **su cumpleaños es el** *his/her birthday is the*			

Author's note: **Don't forget! Tengo/tiene actually means "I have" and "he/she has" in Spanish. You use this verb for telling age. You will see it many times throughout this booklet!* ☺

Unit 2. Saying when my birthday is: VOCABULARY BUILDING

1. Complete with the missing word

a. Me _____ Gonzalo   *My name is Gonzalo*

b. Mi _____ se llama María   *My friend is called María*

c. _____ amigo se llama Jaime   *My friend is called Jaime*

d. Mi _____ es el...   *My birthday is on the...*

e. El _____ de mayo   *The fifth of May*

f. El _____ de noviembre *The 18th November*

g. El cuatro de _____   *The 4th July*

h. _____ cumpleaños es el...   *His/her birthday is on the...*

2. Match up

abril	May
noviembre	my birthday
diciembre	my friend (f)
mayo	April
enero	November
febrero	he/she is called
mi cumpleaños	December
mi amigo	I am called
mi amiga	February
me llamo	January
se llama	my friend (m)

3. Translate into English

a. El catorce de enero

b. El ocho de mayo

c. El siete de febrero

d. El veinte de marzo

e. El diecinueve de agosto

f. El veinticinco de julio

g. El veinticuatro de septiembre

h. El quince de abril

4. Add the missing letter

a. cum__leaños   c. ma__zo   e. a__ril   g. e__ero   i. ju__io   k. d__ciembre

b. fe__rero   d. ma__o   f. jun__o   h. a__osto   j. noviem__re   l. se__tiembre

5. Broken words

a. E___ t_____ d__ e_____   *3rd Jan*

b. E___ c_____ d__ j_____   *5th July*

c. E___ n_____ d__ a_____   *9th Aug*

d. E___ d_____ d__ m_____   *12th March*

e. E___ d_____ d__ a_____   *16th April*

f. E___ d_____ d__ d_____   *19th Dec*

g. E___ v_____ d__ o_____   *20th Oct*

h. E___ v_____ d__ m_____   *24th May*

i. E___ t_____ d__ s_____   *30th Sept*

6. Complete with a suitable word

a. Me _____ Dylan

b. Mi _____ es el dos de mayo

c. Tengo nueve _____

d. Mi _____ se llama Gian

e. Gian _____ diez años

f. Su _____ es el tres de junio

g. Mi _____ es el dieciocho de julio

h. Mi amigo _____ llama Ronan

i. _____ cumpleaños es el cuatro de agosto

j. El ocho de n_____

k. _____ llamo Gabriel García

Unit 2. Saying when my birthday is: READING

Me llamo Rodrigo. Tengo doce años y vivo en México. Mi cumpleaños es el doce de septiembre. Mi amiga se llama Gabriela y tiene catorce años. Su cumpleaños es el veintiocho de mayo. En mi tiempo libre siempre toco la guitarra. ¡Gabriela también!
Mi amiga se llama Carlota. Tiene treinta y cinco años y es profesora. Su cumpleaños es el veintiuno de junio. Carlota tiene un hermano mayor. Su cumpleaños es el ocho de enero.

Me llamo Sergio. Tengo veintidós años y vivo en Lepe, en el sur de España. Mi cumpleaños es el diez de septiembre. Mi amiga se llama Ivana y tiene quince años. Su cumpleaños es el veintiocho de mayo. En mi tiempo libre siempre veo la tele.

Me llamo Mercedes. Tengo siete años y vivo en Santiago, la capital de Chile. Mi cumpleaños es el cinco de diciembre. Tengo dos hermanos, Julio y Enrique. Julio tiene once años y es muy bueno. Su cumpleaños es el treinta de septiembre. Enrique es muy muy malo. Tiene trece años y su cumpleaños es el cinco de enero.

Me llamo Antonio. Tengo ocho años y vivo en Málaga, en Andalucía, en el sur de España. Mi cumpleaños es el nueve de agosto. Mi hermana pequeña tiene cuatro años. Es muy simpática. Su cumpleaños es el nueve de agosto. ¡Igual que yo!

Mi amigo se llama Vidal y tiene diecisiete años. Su cumpleaños es el veinticinco de octubre.

1. Find the Spanish for the following items in Rodrigo's text

a. I am called:

b. I am 12 years old:

c. I live in Mexico:

d. My birthday is:

e. the twelfth of:

f. her birthday is on:

g. in my free time:

h. my friend:

i. is called:

j. she is 35:

k. the 21st of June:

l. has an older brother:

m. the eighth of January:

3. Answer these questions about Mercedes

a. How old is she?

b. Where is Santiago?

c. When is her birthday?

d. How many brothers does she have?

e. Which brother is good?

f. How old in Enrique?

g. When is his birthday?

2. Complete with the missing words

Me llamo Ana. _____ trece

_____ y _____ en Madrid, __

España. _____ un gato en

casa. Mi _____ es

el veintinueve _____ diciembre.

Mi   hermano   _____

nueve _____ y su cumpleaños

es ___ abril.

4. Find Someone Who...

a. ...has a birthday in December

b. ...is 22 years old

c. ...shares a birthday with a sibling

d. ...likes to play the guitar with their friend

e. ...has a friend who is 35 years old

f. ...has a birthday in late September

g. ...has a little sister

h. ...has one good and one bad sibling

i. ...is from the South of Spain

Unit 2. Saying when my birthday is: WRITING

1. Complete with the missing letters

a. Me lla_ _ Paco

b. So_ d_ Bilbao

c. M_ cumpleañ_ _ es el quin_ _ de jun_ _

d. Ten_ _ cat_ _ ce a _ os

e. Mi ami_ a se llam_ Catalina

f. Catalina e_ de Madrid

g. Mi am _ go Miguel e_ d_ Sevilla

h. Miguel tien_ onc_ a_ _s

2. Spot and correct the spelling mistakes

a. Mi cumpleanos es el cuatro de enero

b. Mi llamo Paco

c. Soy di Bilbao

d. Mi amiga se llamo Catalina

e. Catalina tene once años

f. Yo tengo catorse anos

g. Me cumpleaños es el primero de marzo

h. Tengo quinse anos

3. Answer the questions in Spanish

¿Cómo te llamas?

¿Cuántos años tienes?

¿Cuándo es tu cumpleaños?

¿Cuántos años tiene tu hermano/a?

¿Cuándo es su cumpleaños?

4. Write out the dates below in words as shown in the example

a. 15.05 *el quince de mayo*

b. 10.06

c. 20.03

d. 19.02

e. 25.12

f. 01.01

g. 22.11

h. 14.10

5. Guided writing – write 4 short paragraphs in the 1st person singular 'I' describing the people below

Name	Town/City	Age	Birthday	Name of brother	Brother's birthday
Samuel	Sevilla	11	25.12	José	19.02
Ale	Bilbao	14	21.07	Felipe	21.04
Andrés	Gerona	12	01.01	Julián	20.06
Carlos	Valencia	16	02.11	Miguel	12.10

6. Describe this person in the third person:

Name: César

Age: 12

Lives in: Aguadulce

Birthday: 21.06

Brother: Jesús, 16 years old

Birthday: 01.12

Unit 2. Saying when my birthday is: TRANSLATION

1. Faulty translation: spot and correct (in the English) any translation mistakes you find

a. Mi cumpleaños es el veintiocho de abril:
His birthday is on the 27th April

b. Me llamo Roberto y soy de España:
Your name is Roberto and you are from Spain

c. Tengo veintitrés años: *I am 22 years old*

d. Mi amigo se llama Jordi:
My friend I am called Jordi

e. Tiene veintiséis años: *I have 26 years old*

f. Su cumpleaños es el cuatro de abril:
My birthday is the 14th April

2. Translate from Spanish to English

a. el ocho de octubre

b. mi cumpleaños es el...

c. mi amigo se llama...

d. su cumpleaños es el...

e. el once de enero

f. el catorce de febrero

g. el veinticinco de diciembre

h. el ocho de julio

i. el uno de junio

4. Sentence-level translation

a. My name is César. I am 30 years old. I live in Spain. My birthday is on the 11th March.

b. My brother is called Pedro. He is 14 years old. His birthday is on the 18th August.

c. My friend is called Juan. He is 22 years old and his birthday is on the 14th January.

d. My friend is called Angela. She is 18 years old and her birthday is on the 25th July.

e. My friend is called Anthony. He is 20 years old. His birthday is on the 24th September.

3. Phrase-level translation

a. My name is

b. I am ten years old

c. My birthday is the...

d. ...the seventh of May

e. My friend is called Bella

f. she is twelve years old

g. her birthday is the...

h. the 23rd of August

i. the 29th April

Author's note: go back to e. Did you make Bella a girl? "amiga" Well done if you did! ☺

UNIT 3
Describing hair and eyes

In this unit you will learn:

- To describe what a person's hair and eyes are like
- To describe details about their faces (e.g. beard and glasses)
- Colours
- I wear
- He/she wears

You will also revisit:

- Common Spanish names
- The verb "Tener" in the first and third person singular
- Numbers from 1 to 16

UNIT 3
Describing hair and eyes

Me llamo... *I am called* **Se llama** *He/she is called*	Antonio Carlos Diego Emilia Isabel María José Julián Roberto	**y** *and*	**tengo** *I have* **tiene** *he/she has*	**seis años** *6 years* **siete años** *7 years* **ocho años** *8 years* **nueve años** *9 years* **diez años** *10 years* **once años** *11 years* **doce años** *12 years* **trece años** *13 years* **catorce años** *14 years* **quince años** *15 years* **dieciséis años** *16 years*
Tengo el pelo *I have...hair* **Tiene el pelo** *He/she has...hair*	**castaño** *brown* **moreno** *dark brown* **negro** *black* **pelirrojo** *red* **rubio** *blond*	**y**	**a media melena** *medium length* **corto** *short* **en punta** *spiky* **largo** *long* **liso** *straight* **rapado** *very short / crew-cut* **rizado** *curly* **ondulado** *wavy*	
Tengo los ojos *I have... eyes* **Tiene los ojos** *He/she has... eyes*	**azul<u>es</u>** *blue* **marron<u>es</u>** *brown* **verde<u>s</u>** *green* **negro<u>s</u>** *black*	**y**	**(no) llevo** *I don't wear* **(no) lleva** *he/she doesn't wear*	**gafas** *glasses* **bigote** *a moustache* **barba** *a beard*

Unit 3. Describing hair and eyes: VOCABULARY BUILDING

1. Complete with the missing word

a. Tengo el pelo c_____ — *I have brown hair*

b. Tengo el pelo r_____ — *I have blond hair*

c. Llevo _____ — *I wear* a beard*

d. Tengo los ojos a_____ — *I have blue eyes*

e. No llevo g_____ — *I don't wear glasses*

f. Tengo el pelo a med___ mel____ — *I have mid-length hair*

g. Tengo los ojos n_____ — *I have black/dark eyes*

h. Tengo el pelo p_____ — *I have red hair*

2. Match up

El pelo castaño	Brown hair
El pelo negro	Black eyes
El pelo rubio	Moustache
Los ojos negros	Green eyes
Las gafas	Black hair
El bigote	Short hair
Los ojos azules	Long hair
Los ojos verdes	Red hair
El pelo corto	Blonde hair
El pelo largo	Glasses
El pelo pelirrojo	Blue eyes

3. Translate into English

a. El pelo rizado

b. Los ojos azules

c. Llevo gafas

d. El pelo rubio

e. Los ojos verdes

f. El pelo pelirrojo

g. Los ojos negros

h. El pelo moreno

4. Add the missing letter

a. La_go   c. _elo   e. Azu_   g. Riza_o   i. More_o   k. O_os

b. Ga_as   d. Bigo_e   f. V_rdes   h. _iso   j. A media me_ena   l. Lle_o

5. Broken words

a. T_____ e__ p_____ r_____ — *I have curly hair*

b. L_____ g_____ — *I wear glasses*

c. _e_____ _l _____o c_____ — *I have short hair*

d. N__ l_____ b_____ — *I don't have a moustache*

e. _____o ____s o_____ marrones — *I have brown eyes*

f. ____v__ b_____ — *I have a beard*

g. T_____ o_____ a____ — *I am eight years old*

h. M__ l_____ M_____ — *My name is María*

i. _____n__ n_____ a_____ — *I am nine years old*

6. Complete with a suitable word

a. Tengo diez _____

b. _____ barba

c. Me _____ Antonio Ruiz

d. Llevo _____

e. Tengo el _____ liso y corto

f. _____ llevo gafas

g. Tengo ____ ojos marrones

h. Tengo ____ pelo negro

i. No _____ bigote

j. _____ el pelo largo

k. _____ llamo Pedro Sánchez

l. Tengo _____ años

Unit 3. Describing hair and eyes: READING

Me llamo Marta. Tengo doce años y vivo en Buenos aires, la capital de Argentina. Tengo el pelo negro, liso y corto y los ojos azules. Llevo gafas. Mi cumpleaños es el diez de septiembre. Mi hermana tiene el pelo liso. Ella tiene diez años.

Me llamo Inma. Tengo quince años y vivo en La Paz, la capital de Bolivia. Tengo el pelo pelirrojo, ondulado y largo y los ojos azules. No llevo gafas. Mi cumpleaños es el quince de diciembre.

Me llamo Alejandro. Tengo nueve años y vivo en Santiago, la capital de Chile. Tengo el pelo castaño, ondulado y a media melena y los ojos marrones. No llevo gafas. Mi cumpleaños es el cinco de diciembre. Mi hermano se llama Travis. Tiene quince años. Tiene el pelo pelirrojo, largo y liso y los ojos negros. Lleva gafas. Su cumpleaños es el trece de noviembre. Es muy musculoso.

Me llamo Alina. Tengo ocho años y vivo en Quito, la capital de Ecuador. Tengo el pelo castaño, largo y rizado y los ojos verdes. Llevo gafas. Mi cumpleaños es el nueve de mayo. En mi casa tengo tres animales, un caballo, un perro y un gato. Mi hermano se llama Sergio. Tiene catorce años. Tiene el pelo rubio, largo y liso y los ojos verdes, como yo. También lleva gafas, como mi padre. Su cumpleaños es el dos de junio. Es muy inteligente.

Me llamo Pablo. Tengo diez años y vivo en Madrid, la capital de España. Tengo el pelo rubio, liso y corto y los ojos verdes. Llevo gafas. Mi cumpleaños es el ocho de abril.

1. Find the Spanish for the following items in Marta's text

a. I am called:

b. In:

c. I wear glasses:

d. My birthday is:

e. The tenth of:

f. I have:

g. Straight:

h. Black:

i. The eyes:

2. Answer the following questions about Inma's text

a. How old is she?

b. Where is La paz?

c. What colour is her hair?

d. Is her hair wavy, straight or curly?

e. What length is her hair?

f. What colour are her eyes?

g. When is her birthday?

3. Complete with the missing words

Me llamo Pedro. _____ diez años y vivo _____ Caracas, la _____ de Venezuela. Tengo el _____ rubio, liso y corto y los _____ verdes. _____ gafas. Mi cumpleaños ___ el ocho _____ abril.

4. Answer the questions below about all five texts

a. Who has a brother called Sergio?

b. Who is eight years old?

c. Who celebrates their birthday on 9 May?

d. How many people wear glasses?

e. Who has red hair and black-coloured eyes?

f. Who has a very intelligent brother?

g. Whose birthday is in April?

h. Who has brown, wavy hair and brown eyes?

THE LANGUAGE GYM

Unit 3. Describing hair and eyes: TRANSLATION

1. Faulty translation: spot and correct (in the English) any translation mistakes you find

a. Tengo el pelo rubio: *I have black eyes*

b. Tiene los ojos azules: *He/she has brown eyes*

c. Llevo barba: *He has a beard*

d. Se llama Pedro: *I am called Pedro*

e. Tiene el pelo rapado: *I have long hair*

f. Tengo los ojos verdes: *I have green eyes*

g. Vivo en Madrid: *I am from Madrid*

3. Phrase-level translation

a. 'The' blond hair

b. I am called

c. I have

d. 'The' blue eyes

e. 'The' straight hair

f. He/she has

g. Ten years

h. I have black eyes

i. I have nine years

j. 'The' brown eyes

k. 'The' black hair

2. From Spanish to English

a. Tengo el pelo rubio

b. Tengo los ojos negros

c. Tiene el pelo liso

d. Lleva gafas y barba

e. Llevo bigote

f. Llevo gafas de sol

g. No llevo barba

h. Tengo el pelo rizado

i. Tengo el pelo largo

4. Sentence-level translation

a. My name is Mark. I am ten years old. I have black and curly hair and blue eyes.

b. I am twelve years old. I have green eyes and blond, straight hair.

c. I am called Ana. I live in Madrid. I have long blond hair and brown eyes.

d. My name is Pedro. I live in Argentina. I have black hair, very short and wavy.

e. I am fifteen years old. I have black, curly long hair and green eyes.

f. I am thirteen years old. I have red, straight long hair and brown eyes.

Unit 3. Describing hair and eyes: WRITING

1. Split sentences

Tengo el pelo	ojos verdes
Llevo	barba
Tengo los	rubio
Tengo el	y rizado
Tengo el pelo rubio	pelo negro
Me llamo	años
Tengo diez	Marta

2. Rewrite the sentences in the correct order

a. pelo el tengo rizado

b. llevo no barba

c. llamo me Ricardo

d. pelo tengo pelirrojo el

e. se hermano llama Pablo mi

3. Spot and correct the grammar and spelling errors

a. Tengo los ojo negros

b. Mi hermano me llaman Antonio

c. Tiene pelo rizado

d. Se llamo Marta

e. Tengo catorce anos

f. Tengo el liso pelo

g. Tengo el ojos verdes

h. Llevo barbas

i. Llevo gafa

j. Llebo no bigote

4. Anagrams

a. lope pelo

b. rbaba

c. joso

d. soña

e. zulase

f. bioru

g. grosne

h. zadori

5. Guided writing – write 3 short paragraphs in the first person singular 'I' describing the people below

Name	Age	Hair	Eyes	Glasses	Beard	Moustache
Luis	12	Brown Curly Long	Green	Wears	Does not have	Has
Ana	11	Blond Straight Short	Blue	Doesn't wear	Does not have	Does not have
Alejo	10	Red Wavy Medium-length	Black	Wears	Has	Does not have

6. Describe this person in the third person:

Name: Jorge

Age: 15

Hair: Black, curly, very short

Eyes: Brown

Glasses: No

Beard: Yes

 **THE LANGUAGE GYM**

UNIT 4
Saying where I live and am from

In this unit you will learn to talk about:

- Where you live and are from
- If you live in an apartment or a house
- What your accommodation looks like
- Where it is located
- The names of renowned cities and countries in the Hispanic world
- The verb 'I am'

You will also revisit:
- Introducing yourself
- Telling age and birthday

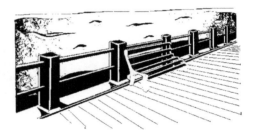

UNIT 4

Saying where I live and am from

Me llamo David y... *My name is David and...*	**vivo en** *I live in*	**una casa** *a house*	**bonita** *pretty* **fea** *ugly* **grande** *big* **pequeña** *small*	**en el centro** *in the centre* **en las afueras** *on the outskirts*
		un piso *a flat*	**en un edificio antiguo** *in an old building* **en un edificio moderno** *in a modern building*	**en la costa** *on the coast*
	soy de *I am from*	Barcelona	**en Cataluña (en España)** *northwest region of Spain*	
		Bilbao	**en el País Vasco (en España)** *northern region of Spain*	
		Bogotá	**en Colombia (la capital)** *capital of Colombia*	
		Buenos Aires	**en Argentina (la capital)** *capital of Argentina*	
		Cádiz	**en Andalucía (en España)** *south of Spain*	
		Cartagena	**en Colombia (en la costa)** *coast of Colombia*	
		La Habana	**en Cuba (la capital)** *capital of Cuba*	
		Lima	**en Perú (la capital)** *capital of Peru*	
		Madrid	**en España (la capital)** *capital of Spain*	
		Quito	**en Ecuador (la capital)** *capital of Ecuador*	
		Santiago	**en Chile (la capital)** *capital of Chile*	
		Montevideo	**en Uruguay (la capital)** *capital of Uruguay*	
		Zaragoza	**en Aragón (en España)** *northern region of Spain*	

Unit 4. Saying where I live and am from: VOCABULARY BUILDING

1. Complete with the missing word

a. Vivo en _____ casa bonita   *I live in a pretty house*

b. Me gusta mi _____   *I like my flat*

c. Soy ___ Madrid   *I am from Madrid*

d. _____ en un piso pequeño   *I live in a small flat*

e. Un piso en un _____ antiguo   *A flat in an old building*

f. _____ de Santiago, la capital de Chile   *I'm from Santiago...*

g. Vivo en una casa _____   *I live in an ugly house*

h. Vivo en las _____   *I live on the outskirts*

2. Match up

el centro	big
bonita	small
grande	old
edificio	pretty
antiguo	the centre
las afueras	the coast
la costa	I am from
España	the outskirts
soy de	ugly
fea	I live in
pequeña	Spain
vivo en	building

3. Translate into English

a. Soy de Argentina

b. Vivo en una casa

c. Mi piso es pequeño

d. Soy de Santiago, en Chile

e. en un edificio moderno

f. Soy de Lima, la capital de Perú

g. Vivo en un piso en la costa de...

h. Soy de Cartagena, en Colombia

4. Add the missing letters

a. Bog__tá   c. Bar_elona   e. Bue__os A_res   g. Car_agena   i. P_ís Vasco

b. Madri_   d. Mon_evideo   f. Z_ragoza   h. Colom_ia   j. C_ba

5. Broken words

a. S_____ d___ l___ H_____ , e___C _____
I am from La Habana, in Cuba

b. V___ e___ u___ c_____ a_____   *I live in an old house*

c. S___ d___ M_____ , l__ c_____ d___ E_____
I am from Madrid, the capital of Spain

d. V_____ e__ u___ p_____ e__ l__ c_____ d__ Chile
I live in a flat on the coast of Chile

e. V_____ e__ u____ c_____ p_____ pero b_____
I live in a small but pretty house

f. S___ d_ M_____ y v_____ e__ u__ e_____
a_____   *I'm from Montevideo and I live in an old building*

g. S___ d___ Q_____   *I am from Quito*

6. Complete with a suitable word

a. Soy ____ Bilbao

b. Vivo ____ un piso bonito

c. En un _____ antiguo

d. Vivo en una casa en el _____

e. Lima es la capital de _____

f. Vivo en una casa _____

g. Soy de _____

h. Vivo en un piso _____

i. Soy de Santiago, en _____

j. Bogotá es la capital de _____

k. Vivo en una casa en la _____

THE LANGUAGE GYM

Unit 4. "Geography test": Using your own knowledge (and a bit of help from Google/your teacher) match the numbers to the cities

Spain	
Num	**City**
	Barcelona
	Bilbao
	Cádiz
	La Coruña
	Madrid

Latin America	
Num	**City**
	Bogotá (Colombia)
	Buenos Aires (Argentina)
	La Habana (Cuba)
	La Paz (Bolivia)
	Lima (Perú)
	Quito (Ecuador)
	México D.F. (México)
	Montevideo (Uruguay)
	Santiago (Chile)

Unit 4. Saying where I live and am from: READING

Me llamo Carlos. Tengo veintidós años y mi cumpleaños es el nueve de agosto. Vivo en Bilbao en el País Vasco en el norte de España. Vivo en una casa bonita en el centro de la ciudad. Tengo dos hermanos, Eduardo y Rubén. Me gusta mucho Eduardo pero Rubén es muy estúpido. Mi amigo José vive en Barcelona, en el noreste de España. Él vive en un piso en un edificio antiguo, también en el centro.

Me llamo Ramón. Tengo quince años y vivo en la Habana, la capital de Cuba. En mi familia somos cuatro personas: mis padres, mi hermano, Guillermo, y yo. Mi cumpleaños es el once de septiembre y Guillermo también. ¡Somos gemelos!

Me llamo Estefanía. Tengo nueve años y vivo en Cartagena, en la costa de Colombia. Vivo en mi casa con mi familia: mis padres, mi hermana mayor, Shakira y yo. Mi cumpleaños es el nueve de mayo y el cumpleaños de Shakira es el treinta de marzo. Ella tiene once años. Mi casa es grande y bonita y está en la costa. ¡Me gusta mucho!

Me llamo Isabela. Tengo veintiún años y vivo en Buenos Aires, la capital de Argentina con mi muy buena amiga, Marina. Vivimos en un piso grande, bonito y moderno en las afueras. Mi cumpleaños es el dos de junio y el cumpleaños de Marina es el doce de julio.

En el piso tengo un perro que se llama Gnarls 'Barkley'. Es muy grande y bueno. Su cumpleaños es el uno de abril. Gnarls 'Barkley' tiene tres años. También tengo una araña, buena pero muy fea, que se llama Luisa. El cumpleaños de mi araña también es el uno de abril. Entonces hago una fiesta para las dos mascotas al mismo tiempo. Es muy práctico.

1. Find the Spanish for the following in Isabela's text

a. My name is

b. I am 21 years old

c. I live in…

d. A big flat

e. On the outskirts

f. The 2nd of june

g. I have a dog

h. He is very big

i. His birthday is on the 1st April

j. He is 3 years old

k. I also have a spider

2. Complete the statements below based on Carlos' text

a. I am _____ years old

b. My birthday is the ____of _____

c. I live in a _____ house

d. My house is in the _____ of town

e. I like Eduardo but Ruben is _____

f. My friend José _____ in Barcelona

g. He lives in an old _____

3. Answer the questions on the four texts above

a. How old is Ramón?

b. Why do Ramón and Guillermo have the same birthday? *(what do you think a 'gemelo' is?)*

c. Who only likes one of his siblings?

d. Who has two pets that share a birthday?

e. Why is it convenient that they share a birthday?

f. Who has a friend that lives in a different city?

g. Who lives with their really good friend?

h. Who does not live in Latin America?

i. Whose birthday is on the twelfth of July?

4. Correct any incorrect statements about Estefanía's text

a. Estefanía vive en Cartagena, en el centro de Colombia

b. En la familia de Estefanía hay *(there are)* cuatro personas

c. Su cumpleaños es en marzo

d. El cumpleaños de Shakira es el tres de marzo

e. Estefanía vive en una casa grande pero fea en la costa

f. Le gusta mucho su casa

 THE LANGUAGE GYM

Unit 4. Saying where I live and am from: TRANSLATION/WRITING

1. Translate into English

a. vivo en

b. una casa

c. un piso

d. bonito

e. grande

f. en un edificio

g. antiguo

h. moderno

i. en el centro

j. en las afueras

k. en la costa

l. soy de

m. en España

n. en Perú

2. Gapped sentences

a. Vivo en una _____ fea   *I live in an ugly house*

b. Un piso en un _____ nuevo   *A flat in a new building*

c. Vivo en un _____ pequeño   *I live in a small flat*

d. Una _____ en las _____   *A house on the outskirts*

e. _____ ___ Madrid   *I am from Madrid*

f. La _____ de España   *The capital of Spain*

3. Complete the sentences with a suitable word

a. Vivo en _____ , la capital de Cuba

b. Soy de Santiago, en _____

c. Vivo en un _____ bonito en las _____

d. Vivo en una casa bonita y _____

e. _____ de Quito, la _____de Ecuador

f. Vivo en un _____ moderno en el centro

4. Phrase-level translation En to Sp

a. I live in…

b. I am from…

c. a house…

d. a flat…

e. ugly (m)…

f. small (m)…

g. in an old building…

h. in the centre…

i. on the outskirts…

j. on the coast…

k. in Catalunya…

5. Sentence-level translation En to Sp

a. I am from Bilbao, in the Basque Country in Spain. I live in a big and pretty house on the outskirts.

b. I am from Buenos Aires, the capital of Argentina. I live in a small and ugly flat in the centre.

c. I am from Montevideo, the capital of Uruguay. I live in a flat in a new building on the coast. My flat is big but ugly.

d. I am from Cádiz in Andalucía, in Spain. I live in a flat in an old building on the outskirts. I like my flat.

THE LANGUAGE GYM

Unit 4. Saying where I live and am from: WRITING

1. Complete with the missing letters

a. Me lla_ _ Paco

b. Vi_ _ en una ca_ _ bon_t_

c. V_v_ en un p_so grand_

d. _ _vo en una _ _sa en el cent_ _

e. So_ de Bogo_ _ en Colom_ _a

f. Yo _oy de Bueno_ Aire_ en Argentin_

g. V_ _ _ en un pis_ peque_o en las afuer_ _

h. _oy de La Haba_ _ en Cu_ _

2. Spot and correct the spelling mistakes

a. Soy de Bogota, en Colombia

b. Vivo en Bilbao en el Pais Basco

c. Vivo en una casa feo

d. Vivo en un piso pequeña

e. Vivo en un moderno edificio

f. Vivo en Andalucia

g. Soy de Barcelona, en Cataluna

h. Soy de Cadiz, en Espana

3. Answer the questions in Spanish

a. ¿Cómo te llamas?

b. ¿Cuántos años tienes?

c. ¿Cuándo es tu cumpleaños?

d. ¿De dónde eres?

e. ¿Dónde vives?

f. ¿Vives en una casa o en un piso?

4. Anagrams (regions of Spain and Latin American countries)

a. hiCel *Chile*

b. luñCataa

c. anlucíadA

d. ubaC

e. rcuaEdo

f. spEaañ

g. erPú

h. loCombia

i. Uguayr

j. nraAgó

5. Guided writing – write 5 short paragraphs in the 1st person singular 'I' describing the people below

Name	Age	Birthday	City	Country or region
Samuel	12	20.06	Buenos Aires	Argentina
Ale	14	14.10	Madrid	Spain
Andrés	11	14.01	Bogotá	Colombia
Carlos	13	17.01	La Habana	Cuba
Nina	15	19.10	Santiago	Chile

6. Describe this person in the third person:

Name: Alejandro

Age: 16

Birthday: 15 May

Country of origin: Quito, Ecuador

Country of residence: Madrid, Spain

 THE LANGUAGE GYM

UNIT 5
Talking about my family members, saying their age and how well I get along with them. Counting to 100.

Revision quickie – Numbers 1-100 / Dates / Birthdays

In this unit you will learn to talk about:

- How many people there are in your family and who they are
- If you get along with them
- Words for family members
- What their age is
- Numbers from 31 to 100

You will also revisit

- Numbers from 1 to 31
- Hair and eyes description

UNIT 5
Talking about my family members, saying their age and how well I get along with them. Counting to 100.

En mi familia está *In my family there is…*	**mi abuelo Jaime** *my grandfather James*		**un**	**año**
	mi padre Juan *my father John*	**Él tiene** *[he has]*	dos tres cuatro cinco seis siete ocho nueve diez	
Hay <u>cuatro</u> personas en mi familia *There are <u>four</u> people in my family…*	**mi tío Iván** *my uncle Ivan*			
	mi hermano mayor / menor Darren *my big/little brother Darren*		once 11 doce 12 trece 13 catorce 14 quince 15	
En mi familia somos <u>cinco</u> *There are five of us in my family*	**mi primo Ian** *my cousin, Ian*			
	mi abuela Adela *my grandmother Adela*		dieciséis 16 diecisiete 17 dieciocho 18 diecinueve 19 veinte 20	**años**
Me llevo bien con… *I get along well with…*	**mi madre Angela** *my mother Angela*			
	mi tía Gina *my aunt Gina*	**Ella tiene** *[she has]*	veintiún 21 veintidós 22 treinta 30 treinta y un 31 treinta y dos 32 cuarenta 40	
Me llevo mal con… *I get along badly with…*	**mi hermana mayor / menor Wendy** *my big/little sister Wendy*		cincuenta 50 sesenta 60 setenta 70 ochenta 80 noventa 90 cien 100	
	mi prima Clara *my girl cousin Clara*			

Author's note: the number one "uno" becomes shortened to "un" before a noun. Watch out for it!

Unit 5. Talking about my family + Counting to 100: VOCAB BUILDING

1. Complete with the missing word

a. En mi f_____ está...   *In my family there is...*

b. Hay_____ personas   *There are five people*

c. Mi _____ , Jaime   *My grandfather, Jaime*

d. Mi abuelo _____ ochenta años   *My grandfather is 80*

e. Mi _____ Angela   *My mother Angela*

f. Ella _____ cincuenta años   *She is 50 years old*

g. Me _____ bien con mi hermano   *I get on well with my bro*

2. Match up

Dieciséis	12
Doce	48
Veintiún	13
Diez	16
Treinta y tres	10
Trece	21
Cuarenta y ocho	15
Cincuenta y dos	5
Cinco	33
Quince	52

3. Translate into English

a. Me llevo mal con...

b. Mi abuela, Adela

c. Mi tío

d. Hay cuatro personas...

e. En mi familia...

f. Me llevo bien con...

g. Mi padre

h. Tiene veinte años

4. Add the missing letter

a. fa_ilia

b. te_go

c. p _rsonas

d. a_uelo

e. he _mano

f. ma_or

g. ma_re

h. p_imo

i. me ll_vo

j. b_en

k. qu_nce

l. die_

5. Broken words

a. H____ s_____ p_____ e__ m__ f_____
There are 6 people in my family

b. M_ h_____ t___ d_____ a_____
My sister is 12 years old

c. E__ m_ fam_ ten_____...   *In my family I have...*

d. M_ p_____ s___ l_____   *My male cousin is called*

e. M_ p_____ t_____ c_____ c_____ a_____ .
My father is 55 years old

f. M_ l_____ m_____c__ m_ h_____ m_____
I get on badly with my older brother...

g. M_ l_____ b_____c__ m_...   *I get on well with my...*

6. Complete with a suitable word

a. En mi _____

b. _____ tres personas

c. Mi hermana _____

d. Tiene catorce _____

e. Mi _____, Gina tiene treinta y cinco años

f. Me llevo _____ con mi padre

g. Hay cuatro _____ en mi familia

h. Me _____ bien con mi abuela

i. No _____ llevo bien con mi tío

j. Mi primo tiene quince _____

k. Me llevo bien _____ mi abuelo

Unit 5. Talking about my family + Counting to 100: VOCABULARY DRILLS

1. Match up

En mi	There are
Familia	In my
Hay	With
Siete	Family
Me llevo bien	I get along well
Con	Seven

2. Complete with the missing word

a. _____ cinco personas — *There are five people*

b. Mi _____, Juan, tiene sesenta años — *My father, John, is 60*

c. Me _____ bien con mi tío — *I get along with my uncle*

d. Me llevo _____ con mi... — *I get along badly with my...*

e. Mi tía, Gina, _____ cuarenta años — *My aunt, Gina, is 40*

f. Él tiene _____ años — *He is 18*

g. _____ tiene veintiséis años — *She is 26*

h. Mi _____, Adela, tiene ochenta años — *My gran, Adela is 80*

3. Translate into English

a. Él tiene nueve años

b. Ella tiene cuarenta años

c. Mi padre tiene cuarenta y cuatro años

d. Me llevo mal con mi abuelo

e. Me llevo bien con mi hermano

f. Mi hermana menor tiene cinco años

g. Hay ocho personas en mi familia

h. En mi familia tengo seis personas

4. Complete with the missing letters

a. Mi hermano m _ _ or *My older brother*

b. En mi fa _ _ lia h _ _ tres personas
In my family there are 3 people

c. Mi primo t _ _ ne dieci _ _ _ o años
My cousin is 18

d. Me _ _evo muy m _ _ con mi hermano
I get along very badly with my brother

e. Mi t_ _ tiene cuarenta _ñ_s
My uncle is 40 years old

f. _ _ llevo muy bi_ _ con mi prima
I get along very well with my cousin

g. Mi pr_ _a t_ _ ne q_ _nce años
My cousin is 15 years old

h. Me llevo regular con _ _ _ _ _
I get along so so with her

i. ¿Cómo e_ _ _ tú? *What are you like?*

5. Translate into Spanish

a. In my family

b. There are

c. My father...

d. is 40 years old

e. I get along well...

f. ...with

6. Spot and correct the errors

a. En mi familia hoy tres personas

b. Mi abela Adela

c. Mi hermano tene nueve años

d. Me lavo mal con mi primo

e. Mi primo tiene ocho anos

f. Mi hermano major, Darren

THE LANGUAGE GYM

Unit 5. Talking about my family + Counting to 100: TRANSLATION

1. Match up

Veinte	30
Treinta	70
Cuarenta	100
Cincuenta	50
Sesenta	20
Ochenta	80
Noventa	40
Cien	60
Setenta	90

3. Write in the missing number

a. Tengo _____ y un años   *I am 31*

b. Mi padre tiene _____ y siete años   *My dad is 57*

c. Mi madre tiene _____ y ocho años   *My mum is 48*

d. Mi abuelo _____ años   *My grandad is 100*

e. Mi tío tiene _____ y dos años   *My uncle is 62*

f. Tienen _____ años   *They are 90*

g. Mis primos tienen _____ y cuatro años   *My cousins are 44*

h. ¿Tiene _____ años?   *Is he/she 70?*

2. Write out in Spanish

a. 35 treinta y cinco

b. 63 s

c. 89 o

d. 74 s

e. 98 n

f. 100 c

g. 82 o

h. 24 v

i. 17 d

4. Correct the translation errors

a. *My father is forty*   mi padre tiene catorce años

b. *My mother is fifty-two*   mi madre tiene cincuenta años

c. *We are forty-two*   tenemos cuarenta dos años

d. *I am forty-one*   tengo treinta y un años

e. *They are thirty-four*   tienen treinta y dos años

5. Translate into Spanish (please write out the numbers in letters)

a. In my family there are 6 people:

b. My mother is called Susana and is 43:

c. My father is called Pedro and is 48:

d. My older sister is called Juanita and is 31:

e. My younger sister is called Amparo and is 18:

f. I am called Arantxa and am 27:

g. My grandfather is called Antonio and is 87:

 **THE LANGUAGE GYM**

Unit 5. Talking about my family + Counting to 100: WRITING

1. Spot and correct the spelling mistakes

a. quarenta   *cuarenta*

b. treintaiuno

c. ocenta y dos

d. veinte y uno

e. nuevanta

f. sien

g. septenta

h. dieciseis

3. Rearrange the sentence below in the correct word order

a. mi En cuatro familia personas hay
In my family there are four people

b. bien con llevo mi No hermano me
I don't get along with my brother

c. padre Mi se llama dos Miguel y cincuenta tiene y años
My father is called Miguel and is fifty-two

d. padre y mi yo En familia mi mi madre, hay personas: tres
In my family there are three people: my mother, my father and I

e. se Mi primo y años Paco siete llama y treinta tiene
My cousin is called Paco and is thirty-seven

f. abuelo, y años Fernando y Mi siete ochenta tiene se llama
My grandfather is called Fernando and is eighty-seven

2. Complete with the missing letters

a. Mi m__dre ti__ne cuar__nta año_

b. Mi pad__e tie__e cin__enta y un a__os

c. Mis abu__los tienen oc__enta añ__s

d. M__ her__ana meno__ t__ene ve__nte añ__ __

e. __i ab__ela t_ _ n __ no__enta a _ _ _ _

f. Mi h__ __m__ __o ma__or t__ __ne treint__ __ñ__ __

4. Complete

a. In my family: E__ m__ f_____

b. There are: H_____

c. Who is called: Q_____ s___ l_____

d. My mother: M__ m_____

e. My father: M__ p_____

f. He is fifty: T_____ c_____ a_____

g. I am sixty: T_____ s_____ a_____

h. He is forty: T_____ c_____ a_____

5. Write a relationship sentence for each person as shown in the example

e.g. Mi mejor amigo, que se llama Paco, tiene quince años

Name	Relationship to me	Age	How I get along with them
e.g. Paco	*Best friend*	*15*	*Very well*
Steve (Smith)	Father	57	Well
Ana	Mother	45	Very badly
Arantxa	Aunt	60	Quite well
Andrés	Uncle	67	Not well
Miquel	Grandfather	75	Very well

Revision Quickie 1:
Numbers 1-100, dates and birthdays, hair and eyes, family

1. Match up

11	quince
12	doce
13	dieciséis
14	dieciocho
15	once
16	diecinueve
17	catorce
18	veinte
19	diecisiete
20	trece

2. Translate the dates into English

a. El treinta de junio

b. El primero de julio

c. El quince de septiembre

d. El veintidós de marzo

e. El treinta y uno de diciembre

f. El cinco de enero

g. El dieciséis de abril

h. El veintinueve de febrero

3. Complete with the missing words

a. Mi cumpleaños _____ el quince de abril

b. Tengo catorce _____

c. Mi hermano _____ el pelo _____

d. ¿De _____ eres?

e. En mi familia _____ cuatro personas

f. _____ madre tiene los _____ marrones

g. Soy _____ Colombia

h. Mi hermano se _____ Roberto

dónde	es	de	tiene	llama
rubio	ojos	años	hay	mi

4. Write out the solution in words as shown in the example

a. cuarenta – treinta diez

b. treinta – diez

c. cuarenta + treinta

d. veinte x dos

e. ochenta – veinte

f. noventa – cincuenta

g. treinta x tres

h. veinte + cincuenta

i. veinte + treinta

5. Complete the words

a. Mi ab _ _ _ _ _   *My grandfather*

b. Mi pr _ _ _ _   *My female cousin*

c. Los oj _ _   *The eyes*

d. Ver _ _ _   *Green*

e. La ba _ _ _   *Beard*

f. Las ga _ _ _   *Glasses*

g. Mi her_ _ _ _ _   *Sister*

h. Te_ _ _   *I have*

6. Translate into English

a. Mi madre tiene el pelo castaño

b. Tengo los ojos azules

c. Tengo cuarenta años

d. Mi abuelo tiene noventa años

e. Mi padre lleva gafas

f. Mi hermano lleva bigote

g. Mi hermano tiene el pelo negro

h. Mi hermana tiene los ojos grises

UNIT 6: (Part 1/2)
Describing myself and another family member (physical and personality)

In this unit you will learn:

- What your immediate family members are like
- Useful adjectives to describe them
- The third person of the verb 'Ser'(to be): 'es' (he is)
- All the persons of the verb 'Tener' in the present indicative

You will also revisit
- Numbers from 1 to 31
- Hair and eyes description

UNIT 6 (Part 1/2)
Intro to describing myself and another family member

		MASCULINE	FEMININE
Yo	**soy**	**alto** *tall* **bajo** *short* **bueno** *good* **delgado** *slim* **feo** *ugly* **fuerte** *strong*	**alta** *tall* **baja** *short* **buena** *good* **delgada** *slim* **fea** *ugly* **fuerte** *strong*
Mi hermana menor *My younger sister* **Mi hermano mayor** *My older brother* **Mi madre** *My mother* **Mi padre** *My father*	**es**	**gordo** *fat* **guapo** *handsome* **musculoso** *muscular* **aburrido** *boring* **antipático** *mean* **divertido** *fun* **generoso** *generous* **malo** *bad* **simpático** *nice* **terco** *stubborn*	**gorda** *fat* **guapa** *pretty* **musculosa** muscular **aburrida** *boring* **antipática** *mean* **divertida** *fun* **generosa** *generous* **mala** *bad* **simpática** *nice* **terca** *stubborn*

Unit 6. Vocabulary building

1. Match

Soy simpático	I am fun
Soy antipático	I am slim
Soy terco	I am generous
Soy guapo	I am mean
Soy divertido	I am nice
Soy generoso	I am short
Soy fuerte	I am strong
Soy malo	I am good-looking
Soy bajo	I am bad
Soy alto	I am tall
Soy delgado	I am stubborn

2. Complete

a. Mi hermano menor es d_____
My younger brother is slim

b. Mi padre es a_____
My father is unfriendly

c. Mi hermana mayor es t_____
My older sister is stubborn

d. Soy m_____ *I am muscular*

e. Mi hermano mayor es d_____
My older brother is fun

f. Mi amigo Paco es f_____ *My friend Paco is strong*

3. Categories – sort the adjectives below in the categories provided

a. fuerte; b. musculoso; c. simpático; d. terco; e. guapo;
f. inteligente; g. paciente; h. malo; i. generoso; j. aburrido;
k. gordo; l. feo; m. divertido

El físico	La personalidad

4. Complete the words

a. Soy aburr_ _ _ (m)

b. No soy f_ _ (m)

c. Soy muscu_ _ _ _ (f)

d. Soy te _ _ _ (m)

e. Soy ma_ _ (f)

f. Soy gua_ _ (m)

g. Soy sim_ _ _ _ _ _ (f)

h. Soy go_ _ _ (m)

5. Translate into English

a. Mi hermana mayor es generosa

b. Mi hermano menor es gordo

c. Mi hermano mayor es aburrido

d. Mi madre es divertida

e. No soy feo

f. Soy un poco terco

g. Soy muy guapo

h. Mi amigo Valentino es fuerte

6. Spot and correct the translation mistakes

a. Soy fuerte: *He is strong*

b. Es gordo: *He is slim*

c. Soy muy guapa: *I am very ugly*

d. Mi madre es alta: *My mother is short*

e. Mi rata es fea: *My rat is small*

f. Mi hermana es terca: *My sister is three*

g. Mi padre es malo: *My father is mean*

8. English to Spanish translation

a. I am strong and funny (f)

b. My mother is very stubborn

c. My sister is short and slim

d. My brother is intelligent

e. I am kind and fun (f)

f. My father is tall and fat

g. Gargamel is ugly and mean

h. I am tall and muscular (m)

7. Complete

a. M_ _ m_ _ _ _ _

b. M_ _ h_ _ _ _ _ _ _

c. M_ _ p_ _ _ _

d. S_ _ _ f_ _ _ _ _

e. E_ _ t_ _ _ _ _

f. S_ _ _ m_ _ _

Grammar Time 1: SER - To be (Part 1)

Masculine		
yo	**soy** *I am*	alto antipático bajo delgado fuerte gordo hablador *[talkative]* paciente simpático
tú	**eres** *you are*	
él **mi hermano** **mi padre**	**es** *he is*	
nosotros **mi padre y yo**	**somos** *we are*	altos antipáticos bajos delgados fuertes gordos habladores pacientes simpáticos
vosotros	**sois** *you guys are*	
ellos **mis hermanos** **mis padres**	**son** *they are*	
Feminine		
yo	**soy** *I am*	alta antipática baja delgada fuerte gorda habladora inteligente paciente simpática
tú	**eres** *you are*	
ella **mi hermana** **mi madre**	**es** *she is*	
nosotras **mi madre y yo**	**somos** *we are*	altas antipáticas bajas delgadas fuertes gordas habladoras inteligentes pacientes simpáticas
vosotras	**sois** *you ladies are*	
ellas **mis hermanas** **mis tías**	**son** *they are*	

Present indicative of "Ser" (to be) – Drills 1

1. Match up

Somos	I am
Son	You are
Soy	He is
Eres	They are
Sois	We are
Es	You guys are

2. Complete with the missing forms of 'Ser'

a. (yo) _____ muy hablador — *I am very talkative*

b. Mi madre _____ divertida — *My mother is funny*

c. Mis hermanas _____ habladoras — *My sisters are talkative*

d. Mi perro _____ muy perezoso — *My dog is very lazy*

e. Mis padres _____ estrictos — *My parents are strict*

f. ¿Cómo _____ tú? — *What are you like?*

g. ¿Cómo _____ tu pelo? — *What is your hair like?*

h. ¡Vosotros _____ muy fuertes! — *You guys are very strong!*

3. Translate into English

a. Mi padre es simpático

b. Mi madre es habladora

c. Mis hermanos son tímidos

d. Mi hermana menor no es muy alta

e. Mi mejor amigo es muy gordo

f. Mi abuelo es muy amable

g. Mi hermana mayor es muy alta

h. ¡Vosotros sois muy fuertes!

4. Complete with the missing letters

a. Nosotros som _ _ muy amables
We are very friendly

b. Mi madre e _ muy estricta *My mother is very strict*

c. Mis padres s _ _ muy pacientes
My parents are very patient

d. Mis primos s _ _ muy antipáticos
My cousins are very unfriendly

e. Mi gato e _ muy gordo *My cat is very fat*

f. ¡Vosotros s _ _ _ muy habladores!
You guys are very talkative

g. S _ _ un poco tímido *I am a bit shy*

h. Mis abuelos s _ _ muy amables
My grandparents are very kind

i. ¿Cómo e _ tu padre? *What is your dad like?*

5. Translate into Spanish

a. You are: (tú) _ _ _ _

b. He is: (él) _ _

c. You guys are: (vosotros) _ _ _ _ _

d. They (f) are: (ellas) _ _ _

e. We (f) are: (nosotras) _ _ _ _ _ _

f. She is: (ella) _ _

6. Spot and correct the errors

a. Mi madre eres muy simpática

b. Mis padres es muy pacientes y amables

c. Mi hermana no es pesado

d. Mi hermana y yo son altos

e. ¿Cómo es tú?

Present indicative of "Ser" (to be) – Drills 2

7. Complete with the missing letters

a. So___os altos   *We are tall*

b. Ere__ bajo   *You are short*

c. Mi perro e__ gordo   *My dog is fat*

d. Mis profesores so___ muy buenos
My teachers are very good

e. Er__s muy guapa   *You are very pretty*

f. No s__y tímido   *I am not shy*

g. Mi hermano y yo s__mos muy trabajadores
My brother and I are very hard-working

8. Complete with the missing forms of the verb SER

a. Mi madre _____

b. Mis padres _____

c. (yo) _____

d. (ellas) _____

e. Mi madre y yo _____

f. Mi hermano _____

g. Tú y tus hermanas _____

h. Tú _____

i. Vosotras _____

9. Complete with the missing forms of SER

a. (yo) _____ de Colombia

b. Mi madre _____ muy alta y guapa

c. Mis padres _____ muy estrictos

d. Mi hermano _____ muy amable

e. (yo) _____ un poco gordo

f. (ellas) _____ bajas

g. Mi hermano y yo _____ musculosos

h. Mi primo Marco _____ italiano

10. Translate into Spanish.
Make sure the <u>underlined words</u> have a feminine ending (a) in Spanish

a. My mother is <u>tall</u>

b. My father is short

c. My brother is not ugly

d. My sister is <u>nice</u>

e. My grandfather is strict

f. My grandmother is patient

g. My mother is intelligent

11. English to Spanish translation. Remember that plural adjectives add an 'S' (e.g. *gordo – gordos*). Make sure that the <u>words underlined</u> end in 'as/os', as shown in the example:

a. *My mother and my sister are very <u>**tall**</u>*: Mi madre y mi hermana son muy alt**as**

b. *My sisters are kind and <u>**nice**</u>*:

c. *My parents are very <u>**nice**</u>*:

d. *I (f) am talkative and <u>**lazy**</u>*:

e. *My brother and I are very <u>**tall**</u>*:

f. *My mother and my sister are <u>**beautiful**</u>*:

g. *My girlfriend and her su sister are very <u>**short**</u>*:

Grammar Time 2: TENER – To have (Part 1)
(Present indicative)

yo	**tengo** *I have*		**castaño** *brown*
tú	**tienes** *you have*		**negro** *black*
			pelirrojo *red*
él			**rubio** *blond*
ella		**el pelo** *the hair*	**a media melena** *mid length*
mi hermana	**tiene** *he/she has*		**liso** *straight*
mi hermano			**ondulado** *wavy*
mi madre			**rizado** *curly*
mi padre			**corto** *short*
			largo *long*
nosotros			
nosotras			**azules** *blue*
mi padre y yo	**tenemos** *we have*		**marrones** *brown*
mi madre y yo		**los ojos** *the eyes*	**negros** *black*
vosotros	**tenéis** *you guys have*		**verdes** *green*
ellos, ellas			**grandes** *big*
mis hermanos	**tienen** *they have*		**pequeños** *small*
mis padres			

Verb drills

1. Translate into English

a. Tenemos el pelo negro

b. Tiene el pelo rubio

c. Tienen el pelo muy largo

d. Tienes el pelo muy corto

e. Tienen los ojos verdes

f. Tiene el pelo pelirrojo

g. Tenemos el pelo rizado

2. Spot and correct the mistakes (note: not all sentences are wrong)

a. Mi madre tiene el pelo rubio

b. Mis hermanos tenéis el pelo gris

c. (yo) tiene el pelo largo

d. El tienen el pelo negro

e. (nosotros) tenemos el pelo corta

f. Mis padres tiene el pelo rizado

3. Complete with the missing verb ending

a. (Yo) Ten____ el pelo rubio

b. Mi madre tien____ los ojos azules

c. Mis hermanas tien____ el pelo pelirrojo

d. Mi padre tien____ el pelo gris

e. (Nosotros) Ten_____ el pelo negro

f. Mi abuelo tien____ el pelo blanco

g. Mi madre y yo ten____ el pelo blanco

h. Mi primo tien____ el pelo castaño

i. (Vosotros) ¿Ten____ el pelo largo?

j. Mi hermano y yo ten_____ el pelo rizado

k. Mi amigo Paco tien____ los ojos verdes

l. Mis hermanos tiene____ el pelo corto

m. Yo ten____ el pelo a media melena

n. (Tú) ¿Tien____ el pelo largo como tu madre?

---

4. Complete with: *tiene, tenemos* **or** *tienen*

a. Mi madre _____ el pelo rubio

b. Mis padres _____ los ojos marrones

c. Mi hermana mayor y yo _____ el pelo negro

d. Mis abuelos _____ el pelo negro

e. Mis padres _____ el pelo rubio

f. Mis hermanas _____ el pelo rizado

g. Mi hermana menor y yo _____ el pelo ondulado

h. Mi primo _____ el pelo pelirrojo

i. Mis dos hermanas _____ el pelo liso

j. Mi amiga Nicola y yo _____ los ojos azules

---

5. Translate into Spanish

a. We have black hair

b. You have long hair

c. You guys have blue eyes

d. She has green eyes

e. My father has curly hair

f. My sister has straight hair

g. My uncle has grey hair

h. My grandfather has no hair

i. My father and I have blond hair

j. My uncle Paco has green eyes

---

6. Guided writing: write a text in the first person singular (I) including the details below:

- Say you are 9 years old
- Say you have a brother and a sister
- Say your brother is 15
- Say he has brown, straight, short hair and green eyes
- Say he is tall and handsome
- Say she is 12
- Say she has black, curly, long hair and brown eyes
- Say your parents are short, have dark hair and brown eyes

---

7. Write an 80 to 100 words text in which you describe four relatives, or friends. You must include their:

a. Name
b. Age
c. Hair (colour, length and type)
d. Eye colour
e. If they wear glasses or not
f. Their physical description
g. Their personality description

UNIT 6 (Part 2/2)
Describing my family and saying why I like/dislike them

En mi familia tengo *In my family I have...* **Hay <u>cuatro</u> personas en mi familia** *There are <u>four</u> people in my family...*	**mi abuelo, Jaime** *my grandfather James* **mi padre, Juan** *my father John* **mi tío, Iván** *my uncle Ivan* **mi hermano mayor /menor, Darren** *my big/little brother Darren* **mi primo, Ian** *my cousin, Ian*	**Me gusta mi ____ porque es...** *I like my ____ because he is...* **Mi padre es bastante...** *My dad is quite...* **Mi padre es muy ...** *My dad is very...* **Mi padre también es un poco...** *My dad is also a bit ...*	**alto** *tall* **bajo** *short* **bueno** *good* **delgado** *slim* **fuerte** *strong* **gordo** *fat* **guapo** *handsome* **antipático** *mean* **divertido** *fun* **generoso** *generous* **inteligente** *clever* **simpático** *nice* **terco** *stubborn*
Me llevo bien con... *I get along well with...* **Me llevo mal con...** *I get along badly with...*	**mi abuela, Adela** *my grandmother Adela* **mi madre, Angela** *my mother Angela* **mi tía, Gina** *my aunt Gina* **mi hermana mayor /menor, Wendy** *my big/little sister Wendy* **mi prima, Clara** *my cousin Clara*	**Me gusta mi ____ porque es...** *I like my ____ because she is...* **Mi madre es bastante...** *My mum is quite...* **Mi madre es muy...** *My mum is very...* **Mi madre también es un poco...** *My mum is also a bit ...*	**alta** *tall* **baja** *short* **buena** *good* **delgada** *slim* **fuerte** *strong* **gorda** *fat* **guapa** *pretty* **antipática** *mean* **divertida** *fun* **generosa** *generous* **inteligente** *clever* **simpática** *nice* **terca** *stubborn*

Unit 6. Describing my family: VOCABULARY BUILDING

1. Complete with the missing word

a. En mi familia t_____   *In my family I have...*

b. Tengo_____ personas   *I have four people...*

c. Mi _____ , Angela   *My mother, Angela*

d. Me llevo _____ con   *I get along well with*

e. Me llevo _____ con   *I get along badly with*

f. Mi tío ____ muy alto   *My uncle is very tall*

g. Mi _____ es muy simpática...   *My aunt is very nice*

h. Mi prima Clara es _____   *My cousin Clara is fun*

2. Match up

Mi tía	My cousin (f)
Mi abuelo	My granddad
Mi madre	My mum
Mi padre	My dad
Mi hermano mayor	My aunt
Mi primo	My little bro
Mi hermano menor	My big bro
Mi tío	My uncle
Mi hermana	My sister
Mi prima	My cousin (m)

3. Translate into English

a. Me gusta mi tío

b. Mi prima es generosa

c. Tiene el pelo rubio

d. Me llevo bien con...

e. No me gusta mi...

f. Me llevo mal con...

g. Es terco

h. Es tranquila

4. Add the missing letter

a. Te_co   c. _impático   e. _rimo   g. Ma_or   i. Tambié_   k. Me gus_a

b. Me ll_vo   d. _buelo   f. _enor   h. M_dre   j. _ío   l. Por_ue

5. Broken words

a. E__ m__ fam__ ten_____...

In my family I have...

b. C_____ p_____

Four people

c. M__ m_____ e__ m_____ s_____

My mother is very nice

d. M__ l_____ b_____ c____ m__...

I get on well with my...

e. M__ t_____ e__ m_____ g_____

My uncle is very generous

f. M__ l_____ m_____ c____ m__...

I get on badly with my...

g. M__ h_____ t_____ e__ p_____ l_____

My sister has long hair

h. M__ p_____ e__ b_____ i_____

My father is quite clever

6. Complete with a suitable word

a. Tengo cuatro_____

b. _____ simpática

c. Me _____ bien

d. Es muy _____

e. Tiene el _____ rubio

f. ____ gusta mi madre

g. Me llevo _____ con mi tío

h. Tiene el pelo negro y _____

i. Tiene los _____ azules

j. Mi primo es _____ divertido

k. Mi _____ es muy inteligente

l. Mi abuela tiene ochenta _____

Unit 6. Describing my family: READING

Soy Carlos. Tengo diez años y vivo en Kuala Lumpur, la capital de Malasia. En mi familia tengo cinco personas, mi padre Juan, mi madre Angela y mis dos hermanos, Darren y Pedro. Me llevo muy bien con Darren porque es simpático y generoso. Sin embargo, me llevo mal con Pedro porque es muy malo.

Me llamo Verónica. Tengo catorce años y vivo en Marbella, en el sur de España. Me gusta mucho mi abuelo porque es muy divertido. Es inteligente pero muy tímido.
Mi padre, es muy gordo y muy terco. Tiene los ojos marrones y el pelo rapado.

Me llamo Manolo. Tengo quince años y vivo en Galicia, en el noroeste de España. Tengo el pelo rubio y rapado. En mi familia tengo seis personas. No me llevo bien con mi hermana porque es estúpida y terca. Me llevo muy bien con mis primos porque son muy simpáticos.
Mi primo favorito se llama Ian y es alto, grande y fuerte. Es muy divertido y simpático. Tiene el pelo moreno y corto y lleva gafas.

Soy Pedro Sanchez. Tengo diez años y vivo en Madrid, la capital de España. Soy muy muy guapo. En mi familia tengo muchas personas, ocho en total. Me gusta mi tío pero no me gusta mi tía. Me llevo muy bien con mi tío César porque es divertido y simpático. Sin embargo, mi tía es antipática y horrible.
Mi tía María tiene el pelo rubio, largo y rizado y los ojos azules como yo. Su cumpleaños es el cinco de mayo.

Me llamo Juanjo. Tengo nueve años y vivo en Toledo, en España. En mi familia tengo cuatro personas. Me llevo mal con mi padre porque es muy terco y antipático. Me gusta mucho mi abuela porque es muy buena.

1. Find the Spanish for the following items in Verónica's text

a. I am called:

b. in the south:

c. my grandfather:

d. but:

e. very:

f. my father:

g. brown eyes:

h. very short hair:

2. Answer the following questions about Pedro

a. How old is he?

b. Where is he from?

c. How many people are there in his family?

d. Who does he get along well with?

e. Why does he like César?

f. Who does he not like?

g. When is her birthday?

3. Complete with the missing words

Me llamo Alejandra. _____ diez años y vivo _____ Barcelona. En mi familia tengo cuatro _____.

Me _____ bien con mi abuelo porque _____ muy simpático y bueno. Mi padre tiene el _____ corto y los _____ verdes.

4. Find Someone Who...

a. ...has a granny who is very good

b. ...is fifteen years old

c. ...celebrates their birthday on 5th May

d. ...has a favourite cousin

e. ...is from the south of Spain

f. ...only gets along well with one of his brothers

g. ...has a shaved head and very short hair

h. ...is a bit arrogant

i. ...has green eyes

Unit 6. Describing my family: TRANSLATION

1. Faulty translation: spot and correct any translation mistakes (in the English)

a. En mi familia tengo cuatro personas: *In my family I have fourteen people*

b. Mi madre, Angela y mi hermano Darren: *My mother Angela and my cousin Darren*

c. Me llevo muy mal con mi padre: *I get on very well with my father*

d. Mi tío se llama Iván: *My father is called Ivan*

e. Iván es muy simpático y divertido: *Ivan is very mean and fun*

f. Iván tiene el pelo rapado: *Ivan has long hair*

3. Phrase-level translation

a. He is nice

b. She is generous

c. I get along well with...

d. I get along badly with...

e. My uncle is fun

f. My little brother

g. I like my cousin Mary

h. She has short and black hair

i. He has blue eyes

j. I don't like my granddad

k. He is very stubborn

2. From Spanish to English

a. Me gusta mi abuelo

b. Mi abuela es muy buena

c. Mi primo tiene el pelo rapado

d. Me llevo bien con mi hermano mayor

e. Me llevo muy mal con mi prima

f. Me gusta mi abuelo porque es generoso

g. Mi padre es simpático y divertido

h. No me gusta mi hermano menor

i. Me llevo mal con mi primo Ernesto porque es estúpido

4. Sentence-level translation

a. My name is Pedro Sánchez. I am nine years old. In my family I have four people.

b. My name is Carla. I have blue eyes. I get along well with my brother.

c. I get along badly with my brother because he is stubborn.

d. My name is Frank. I live in Spain. I do not like my uncle David because he is mean.

e. I like my cousin a lot because she is very good.

f. In my family I have five people. I like my father but I do not like my mother.

Unit 6. Describing my family: WRITING

1. Split sentences

Mi padre es	pelo negro
Mi madre es	bien con
Tiene los	mi tío
Tiene el	simpático
No me gusta	ojos negros
Me gusta mucho mi	generosa
Me llevo	tía

2. Rewrite the sentences in the correct order

a. en mi seis tengo familia personas

b. me con mi llevo bien hermano

c. no mi me gusta tío

d. mi los ojos madre tiene azules

e. mi y simpática tía es divertida

f. ojos los tengo negros

3. Spot and correct the grammar and spelling errors

a. En mi familia tengos

b. Me lleva bien con…

c. No me gusto mi tía…

d. Mi hermana es divertido

e. Me llevo malo con…

f. Mi padre es generosa

g. Tiene los ojo azul

h. Mi hermana es muy malo

i. Tiene el pelo rapados

j. Mi gusta mucho mi abuela

4. Anagrams

a. fimalia

b. deadlga

c. groda

d. pagua

e. inligteente

f. mispática

g. treco

h. verditida

5. Guided writing – write 3 short paragraphs describing the people below in the first person:

Name	Age	Family	Likes	Likes	Dislikes
Paco	12	4 people	Mother because very nice. Has long blond hair.	Older brother because fun and very good.	Cousin Gemma because very mean and bad.
Leo	11	5 people	Father because very fun. Has short black hair.	Grandmother because very nice and generous.	Uncle Eduardo because stubborn and ugly.
Miguel	10	3 people	Grandfather because very funny. Has very short hair.	Younger sister because very good and relaxed.	Aunt Carolina because very strong but stubborn.

6. Describe this person in the third person:

Name: Uncle Antonio
Hair: Blond, crew-cut
Eyes: Blue
Opinion: Like a lot
Physical: Tall and strong
Personality: Nice, fun, generous.

UNIT 7
Talking about pets

Grammar Time: TENER (pets and description)
Questions skills: Age / Descriptions / Pets

In this unit will learn how to say in Spanish

- What pets you have at home
- What pet you would like to have
- What their name is
- Some more adjectives to describe appearance and personality
- Key question words

You will also learn how to ask questions about
- Name / age / appearance / quantity

You will revisit the following
- Introducing oneself
- Family members
- Describing people
- The verb 'Tener' (to have) in the present indicative

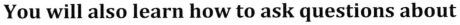

UNIT 7
Talking about pets

En casa tengo *At home I have* **No tengo** *I don't have* **Mi amigo Paco tiene…** *My friend Paco has…*	**un mono** *a monkey*	**que se llama Alfonso** *that is called Alfonso*
	un caballo *a horse* **un conejo** *a rabbit* **un gato** *a cat* **un hámster** *a hamster* **un loro** *a parrot* **un pájaro** *a bird* **un pato** *a duck* **un perro** *a dog* **un pez** *a fish* **un pingüino** *a penguin* **un ratón** *a mouse*	**pequeño** *small* **grande** *big* **amarillo** *yellow* **azul** *blue* **blanco** *white* **naranja** *orange* **rojo** *red* **verde** *green* **aburrido** *boring* **bonito** *pretty* **cariñoso** *affectionate* **divertido** *fun* **feo** *ugly* **gracioso** *funny* **vivaz** *lively*
	una gallina *a chicken*	**que se llama Nayali** *that is called Nayali*
	una araña *a spider* **una cobaya** *a guinea pig* **una rata** *a rat* **una serpiente** *a snake* **una tortuga** *a turtle*	**pequeña** *small* **grande** *big* **amarilla** *yellow* **azul** *blue* **naranja** *orange* **negra** *black* **roja** *red* **verde** *green* **aburrida** *boring* **bonita** *pretty* **cariñosa** *affectionate* **divertida** *fun* **fea** *ugly* **graciosa** *funny* **vivaz** *lively*
Me gustaría tener *I'd like to have* **No me gustaría tener** *I wouldn't like to have*	**un gato** *a cat* **una tortuga** *a turtle*	

Unit 7. Talking about pets: VOCABULARY BUILDING

1. Complete with the missing word

a. En casa tengo un p_____   *At home I have a bird*

b. No tengo un c_____   *I don't have a rabbit*

c. Me gustaría tener un p_____   *I'd like to have a dog*

d. Me gustaría tener una t_____   *I would like to have a turtle*

e. En c_____ tengo un g_____   *At home I have a cat*

f. No tengo una s_____   *I don't have a snake*

g. T_____ una araña en casa   *I have a spider at home*

h. Me g_____ tener un hámster   *I'd like to have a hamster*

2. Match up

un gato	a rat
un perro	a hamster
un caballo	two fish
un pájaro	a cat
un pez	a turtle
una tortuga	a fish
un hámster	a guinea pig
un loro	a dog
dos peces	a parrot
una rata	a bird
una cobaya	a horse

3. Translate into English

a. Tengo un perro

b. Mi amiga Lina tiene un ratón

c. Tengo dos peces

d. No tengo animales en casa

e. Tengo tres perros

f. Me gustaría tener una cobaya

g. Mi hermano tiene una tortuga

h. Mi gato tiene cinco años

4. Add the missing letter

a. Mi am__go

b. Una tortu_a

c. Un _oro

d. Dos pe__es

e. Un pe__

f. Una _ata

g. Una coba_a

h. Un p_jaro

5. Anagrams

a. rroep perro

b. atgo

c. tugator

d. epz

e. olro

f. rpitenees

g. ñaraa

h. yaboca

6. Broken words

a. E__ c_____ t_____ u__ p_____

At home I have a dog

b. M_ a____ Pablo t_____ u__ l_____

My friend Pablo has a parrot

c. M_ h_____ t_____ u___ t_____

My brother has a turtle

d. N__ t_____ u__ c_____   *I don't have a rabbit*

e. T_____ u____ s_____   *I have a snake*

f. Alejandro t_____ u__ g_____   *Alejandro has a cat*

g. T_____ u__ p_____ a_____   *I have a blue fish*

h. T_____ d_____ a_____   *I have two animals*

7. Complete with a suitable word

a. Tengo diez _____

b. Mi pez se _____ Rex

c. Mi _____ Pablo tiene un loro

d. Mi hermano _____ una rata

e. En _____ tengo dos mascotas

f. _____casa tengo dos mascotas, un perro y una _____

g. En casa tengo _____ cobaya

h. En casa tengo _____ pájaro

i. Mi hermana _____ un caballo

j. Mi _____ es blanco y marrón

Unit 7. Talking about pets: READING

Me llamo Elena. Tengo ocho años y vivo en Madrid. En mi familia hay cuatro personas: mis padres y mi hermano menor, que se llama Miguel. Miguel es muy antipático y pesado. Tenemos dos mascotas: un perro que se llama Bueno y un gato que se llama Malo. Bueno es muy cariñoso. Malo es muy antipático. ¡Igual que mi hermano!

Me llamo Roberto. Tengo nueve años y vivo en Málaga. En mi familia hay cuatro personas: mis padres y mi hermano mayor, que se llama Francisco. Él tiene doce años y es muy divertido. Tenemos dos mascotas: un loro que se llama Rico y un gato que se llama Pau. Rico es muy hablador. Pau es muy juguetón, igual que mi hermano.

Me llamo Julio. Tengo nueve años y vivo en Buenos Aires. En mi familia hay cinco personas: mis padres y mis dos hermanos, que se llaman Jorge y Manuel. Jorge es muy hablador y gracioso. Manuel es muy serio y trabajador. Tenemos dos mascotas en casa: una cobaya que se llama Sam y una tortuga que se llama Despacito. La cobaya es muy divertida y vivaz. Despacito es muy serio, igual que mi hermano Manuel.

5. Fill in the blanks

Me l_____ Paco. Tengo once a_____ y v_____ en Barcelona. En mi c_____ hay cinco personas: mis padres y m____ dos hermanas, que se l_____ Ale y Marta. Ale e____ muy habladora y amable. Marta es m_____ perezosa ____ antipática. T_____ dos mascotas en casa: una rata q_____ se llama Maya y una gata que s____ llama Swift. Es m____ divertida y vivaz. Maya e____ muy amable, i_____ q_____ mi h_____ Marta.

Me llamo Selene. Tengo diez años. En mi familia hay cuatro personas: mis padres y mis dos hermanas menores, que se llaman Sabrina y Luz. Sabrina es muy generosa y servicial. Luz es muy terca y aburrida. Tenemos dos mascotas: un conejo que se llama Busy y un pato que se llama Loco. Busy es muy tranquilo y amable. Loco es muy ruidoso y vivaz *(lively)*. ¡Igual que mi hermano!

1. Find the Spanish in Elena's text

a. two pets

b. which is called

c. a cat

d. a dog

e. very affectionate

f. like my brother

g. my parents

h. my name is

i. very unfriendly

j. four people

2. Find Someone Who...

a. ...has a cat

b. ...has a parrot

c. ...has a duck

d. ...has a guinea pig

e. ...has a rabbit

f. ...has a dog

3. Answer the following questions about Julio's text

a. Where does Julio live?

b. What is his brother Manuel like?

c. Who is fun and lively?

d. Who is like Manuel?

e. Who is Jorge?

f. Who is Despacito?

g. Who is Sam?

4. Fill in the table below

Name	Elena	Roberto
Age		
City		
Pets		
Description of pets		

 THE LANGUAGE GYM

Unit 7. Talking about pets: TRANSLATION

1. Faulty translation: spot and correct any translation mistakes you find below

a. En mi familia hay cuatro personas y dos mascotas *In my family there are four people and three pets.*

b. En casa tenemos dos mascotas: un perro y una rata *At home we have two pets: a dog and a rabbit*

c. Mi amigo Paco tiene una tortuga que se llama Speedy. Speedy es muy graciosa *My friend Paco has a duck called Speedy. Speedy is very boring.*

d. Mi hermano tiene un caballo que se llama Dylan *My sister has a parrot called Dylan*

e. My madre tiene una cobaya que se llama Nicole *My father has a frog called Nicole*

f. Tengo un gato que se llama Sleepy. Sleepy es muy vivaz *I have a dog called Sleepy. Sleepy is very beautiful*

2. Translate into English

a. Un gato divertido

b. Un perro cariñoso

c. Un pato gracioso

d. Una tortuga aburrida

e. Un caballo hermoso

f. Una rata vivaz

g. Una cobaya curiosa

h. Tengo dos mascotas

i. En casa no tenemos mascotas

j. Me gustaría tener un perro

k. Me gustaría tener un pez

l. Tengo un hámster, pero me gustaría tener una serpiente

3. Phrase-level translation En to Sp

a. A boring dog

b. A lively duck

c. At home

d. We have

e. A beautiful horse

f. A curious cat

g. I have

h. I don't have

i. I would like to have

4. Sentence-level translation En to Sp

a. My brother has a horse who is called Rayo.

b. My sister has an ugly turtle who is called Nicole.

c. I have a fat hamster called Gordito

d. At home we have three pets: a duck, a rabbit and a parrot.

e. I have a rat called Stuart

f. At home we have three pets: a cat, a dog and a hamster

g. I have two fish which are called Nemo and Dory

Unit 7. Talking about pets: WRITING

1. Split sentences

Tengo un perro que	blanca
En casa tenemos	tener una araña
Tengo una rata	se llama Speedy
Tengo un gato	cobaya
Me gustaría	dos mascotas
Mi hermano tiene una	casa
No tengo animales en	negro

2. Rewrite the sentences in the correct order

a. mascotas tenemos En tres casa

b. una gustaría tener Me rata

c. un Tengo gato un perro y

d. cobaya amigo negra Mi tiene Pablo una

e. Fran verde un que Tenemos se pájaro llama

f. dos Tenemos azules peces

g. tiene llama hermana un que se Mi loro Nicole

3. Spot and correct the grammar and spelling note: in several cases a word is missing

a. En casa un perro un gato

b. Tengo una cobaya negro

c. Me gustaría tener serpiente

d. Mi hermana tengo una gata blanca

e. Mi amigo Pedro tiene dos pez

f. Mi caballo me llama Graham

g. Tengo una caballo negro

h. En casa tenemos dos mascota

4. Anagrams

a. rrope

b. toga

c. tara

d. aopt

e. enjoco

f. bacoya

g. scomaast

6. Describe this person in the third person:

Name: Roberto

Hair: Blond, short

Eyes: Green

Personality: Very nice

Physical: Short, fat

Pets: A dog, a cat and two fish and would like to have a spider

5. Guided writing – write 3 short paragraphs (in 1st person) describing the pets below

Name	Animal	Age	Colour	Character or appearance
Paco	Dog	4	White	Affectionate
Leo	Duck	6	Blue	Funny
Miguel	Horse	1	Brown	Beautiful

Grammar Time 3: TENER (Part 2)
(Pets and description)

1. Translate

a. I have: t _ _ _ _

b. You have: t _ _ _ _ _

c. She has: t _ _ _ _

d. We have: t _ _ _ _ _ _

e. You guys have: t _ _ _ _ _

f. They have: t _ _ _ _ _

2. Translate into English

a. Tengo un caballo muy hermoso. Se llama Paco.

b. Mi hermano tiene un gato muy feo.

c. Mi madre tiene un perro muy divertido.

d. Mis primos tienen una cobaya muy gorda.

e. En casa tenemos un pato muy ruidoso.

f. Mi amigo Javier tiene una tortuga muy grande .

3. Complete

a. *I have a guinea pig*   T_____ una cobaya

b. *It is two years old*   T_____ dos años

c. *We have a turtle. It is 4 years old*   T_____ una tortuga. T_____ cuatro años

d. *My sister has a dog*   Mi hermana t_____ un perro

e. *My uncles have two cats*   Mis tíos t_____ dos gatos

f. *They are three years old*   T_____ tres años

g. *My brother and I have a snake*   Mi hermano y yo t_____ una serpiente

h. *Do you guys have pets?*   ¿T_____ mascotas?

i. *What animals do you have?*   ¿Qué animales t_____?

4. Translate into Spanish

a. I have a guinea pig. It is three years old.

b. We don't have pets at home.

c. My dog is three years old. It is very big.

d. I have three brothers. They are very mean.

e. My cousins have a duck and a guinea pig.

f. My auntie has blond, curly and long hair. She is very pretty.

g. My brother and I have black hair and green eyes.

Question Skills 1: Age / Descriptions / Pets

1. Match question and answer

¿Cuántos años tienes?	Tienen ochenta años
¿Por qué no te llevas bien con tu madre?	Estoy bien, gracias
¿Cómo es tu pelo?	Tengo quince años
¿Cuántos años tienen tus abuelos?	Es el azul
¿De qué color tienes los ojos?	Porque es muy estricta
¿Cuál es tu color preferido?	Es el perro
¿Cómo estás?	No, no tengo
¿Tienes mascotas?	Es pelirrojo
¿Cuál es tu animal preferido?	El veinte de junio
¿Cuántas mascotas tienes?	No, porque es muy serio y perezoso
¿Cómo eres de carácter?	Son azules
¿Cómo eres físicamente?	Tengo dos. Un gato y un loro
¿Te llevas bien con tu padre?	Soy simpático y hablador
¿Cuándo es tu cumpleaños?	Soy bajo y un poco gordo

2. Complete with the missing words

a. ¿De _____ eres?
Where are you from?

b. ¿_____ eres de carácter?
What are you like in terms of character?

c. ¿_____años tiene tu padre?
How old is your father?

d. ¿Te _____ bien con tu madre?
Do you get along with your mum?

e. ¿_____ es tu cumple?
When is your birthday?

f. ¿_____ es tu perro?
What is your dog like?

g. ¿_____ mascotas tienes?
How many pets do you have?

3. Translate the following question words into English

a. ¿Cuál?

b. ¿Cuándo?

c. ¿Dónde?

d. ¿Cómo?

e. ¿De dónde?

f. ¿Quién?

g. ¿Cuánto?

h. ¿Cuántos?

i. ¿Por qué?

5. Translate into Spanish

a. What is your name?

b. How old are you?

c. What is your hair like?

d. What is your favourite animal?

e. Do you get along with your father?

f. Why don't you get along with your mother?

g. How many pets do you have?

h. Where are you from?

4. Complete

a. ¿C_____ a_____ tienes?

b. ¿D__ d_____ eres?

c. ¿C_____ e__ t__ p_____?

d. ¿C_____ e____ d__ c_____?

e. ¿C_____ m_____ tienes?

f. C_____ e__ t__ c_____?

g. ¿T__ l_____ b____ c___ t__ p_____?

 **THE LANGUAGE GYM**

53

UNIT 8
Saying what jobs people do, why they like/dislike them and where they work

Grammar Time: -Ar verbs like trabajar + SER

In this unit will learn how to say:

- What jobs people do
- Why they like/dislike those jobs
- Where they work
- Adjectives to describe jobs
- Words for useful jobs
- Words for types of buildings
- The full conjugation of the verb 'Trabajar' (to work) in the present indicative

You will revisit the following:
- Family members
- The full conjugation of the verb 'Ser' (to be)
- Description of people and pets

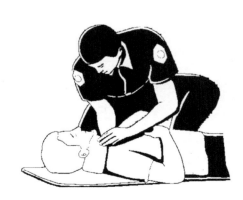

UNIT 8
Saying what jobs people do, why they like/dislike them and where they work

Mi padre *My father*	**es** *he is*	**actor** *actor* **abogado** *lawyer* **amo de casa** *house-husband* **cocinero** *chef* **contable** *accountant*		**aburrido** *boring*	**Trabaja en…** *he/she works in…* ...**el campo** *the countryside* ...**casa** *at home*
Mi hermano menor *My younger brother*	**trabaja como** *works as a*	**enfermero** *nurse* **granjero** *farmer* **hombre de negocios** *business man* **ingeniero** *engineer*	**le gusta porque es** *he/she likes it because it is*	**activo** *active* **difícil** *difficult*	...**la ciudad** *the city* ...**un colegio** *a school*
Mi tío *My uncle*		**mecánico** *mechanic* **médico** *doctor* **peluquero** *hairdresser* **profesor** *teacher*	**no le gusta porque es** *he/she doesn't like it because it is*	**divertido** *fun* **estimulante** *exciting*	...**una empresa** *a company* ...**un garaje** *a garage*
Mi madre *My mother*	**es** *she is*	**actriz** *actress* **abogada** *lawyer* **ama de casa** *house-wife* **cocinera** *chef* **contable** *accountant*	**le encanta porque es** *he/she loves it because it is*	**estresante** *stressful* **fácil** *easy*	... **una granja** *a farm* ...**un hotel** *a hotel* ...**una oficina** *an office*
Mi hermana mayor *My older sister*	**trabaja como** *works as a*	**enfermera** *nurse* **granjera** *farmer* **ingeniera** *engineer* **mujer de negocios** *business woman* **mecánica** *mechanic*	**lo odia porque es** *he/she hates it because it is*	**gratificante** *rewarding* **interesante** *interesting*	...**un restaurante** *a restaurant* ...**un taller** *a workshop*
Mi tía *My aunt*		**médica** *doctor* **peluquera** *hairdresser* **profesora** *teacher*			...**un teatro** *a theatre*

Unit 8. Saying what jobs people do: VOCABULARY BUILDING

1. Complete with the missing word

a. Mi padre es _____ *My father is a lawyer*

b. Mi tía es _____ *My aunt is a hairdresser*

c. Mi hermano menor trabaja como _____
My younger brother works as a mechanic

d. Mi madre es _____ *My mother is a doctor*

e. Mi hermana _____ trabaja como _____
My older sister works as an engineer

f. Mi tía es _____ *My aunt is an accountant*

g. Mi _____ es _____ *My uncle is a farmer*

2. Match up

es aburrido	it's stressful
es activo	it's fun
es difícil	it's hard
es divertido	it's active
es estimulante	it's rewarding
es estresante	it's boring
es fácil	it's interesting
es gratificante	it's easy
es interesante	it's exciting

3. Translate into English

a. Mi madre es mecánica

b. Le gusta su trabajo

c. Trabaja en un garaje

d. Mi hermano es contable

e. No le gusta su trabajo

f. Mi primo es peluquero

g. Le encanta su trabajo

h. Porque es divertido

4. Add the missing letter

a. Es f__cil

b. L__ gusta

c. Ing__niera

d. __édico

e. Es e__tresante

f. T__abaja como

g. Es en__ermera

h. Mi t__o

5. Anagrams

a. anerGrjo

b. ogAbado

c. caéMdi

d. rotcA

e. rAizct

f. Coblenta

g. Peuerluqo

h. Aecmadasa

6. Broken words

a. E___ a_____ d__ c_____ *He is a house husband*

b. L__ g_____ s___ t_____ *He likes his job*

c. M__ h_____ e___ g_____ *My bro is a farmer*

d. T_____ *He/she works*

e. E__ e___ c_____ *In the countryside*

f. O_____ s___ t_____ *He hates his job*

g. P_____ e__ a_____ *Because it is active*

h. E____ m__ g_____ *It is very rewarding*

7. Complete with a suitable word

a. Mi madre es _____

b. Le_____ su trabajo

c. Le gusta porque es _____

d. Trabaja en _____

e. Mi _____ es peluquero

f. No _____ gusta su trabajo

g. Porque es muy _____

h. ___ tía es médica

i. Le gusta su _____

j. Mi tío es mecánico, trabaja en un_____

Unit 8. Saying what jobs people do: READING

Me llamo Felipe. Tengo veinte años y vivo en Cartagena, en Colombia. En mi familia hay cuatro personas. Tengo un perro muy divertido, David. Mi padre trabaja como médico, en la ciudad. Le gusta su trabajo porque es gratificante y divertido. Mi tío Daniel es granjero y le encanta su trabajo. A veces, es un trabajo duro y difícil, pero le encantan los animales.

Me llamo Sebastián. En mi familia hay cuatro personas. Mi padre se llama Mateo y es abogado. Le gusta su trabajo porque es interesante. Sin embargo, a veces es estresante. Mi madre es ama de casa y le gusta bastante su trabajo. Dice que es muy gratificante. En casa tengo un perro que se llama Daniel. ¡Es muy grande y divertido! No me gustan los gatos.

Me llamo Samuel. Soy de Valencia. Mi persona favorita en mi familia es mi madre. Es tímida pero muy simpática. Mi madre es ingeniera pero ahora no trabaja. Odio a mi tío, es inteligente pero muy muy antipático. Mi tío es profesor pero odia su trabajo porque es difícil y aburrido. Trabaja en un colegio en Valencia, pero odia a los niños. En casa tengo una tortuga que se llama Speedy. Es lenta pero muy graciosa, igual que mi hermana Casandra.

Me llamo Camila. En mi familia hay cuatro personas. Mi madre se llama Valeria y es peluquera. Le gusta su trabajo porque es interesante y activo. Mi padre es amo de casa pero no le gusta mucho su trabajo porque dice que es muy difícil y un poco aburrido. En casa no tengo un animal pero me gustaría tener un caballo. Mi primo tiene un caballo que se llama Cristián y es muy grande y fuerte. ¡Qué guay!

1. Find the Spanish in Felipe's text

a. I am 20

b. I have a dog

c. my dad works as...

d. a doctor

e. in the city

f. he likes his work

g. it is rewarding

h. sometimes

i. he loves his work

2. Answer the questions on ALL texts

a. Who is Cristián?

b. Whose mum is a housewife?

c. Who has an uncle that is in the wrong job?

d. Whose father is a doctor?

e. Who has a turtle?

f. Who has a dog?

3. Answer the following questions about Samuel

a. Where does Samuel live?

b. Who is his favourite person?

c. What does his mum do 2 details?

d. Why does he hate his uncle?

e. Why is his uncle a bad teacher?

f. Who is Speedy?

g. What is Casandra like?

5. Fill in the blanks

Me l_____ Mariana. Tengo trece a_____ y v_____ en Santiago de Compostela. En mi f_____ hay cinco personas. Mi primo Cristóbal Pye e____ muy hablador y amable, tiene treinta años. Cristóbal es pr_____ y trabaja en un c_____. Vive en Liverpool, en Inglaterra. Le gusta su t_____ porque es int_____ y gra_____. Mi pad___ no trabaja ahora. En casa tengo ___ animal que se lla___ Damián. ¡Es una ara___: una tarántula!

4. Fill in the table below

Name	Mariana	Cristóbal
Age		
City		
Pets/Job		
Opinion of job	- - -	

Unit 8. Saying what jobs people do: TRANSLATION

1. Faulty translation: spot and correct IN THE ENGLISH any translation mistakes you find below

a. Mi padre trabaja como actor y le gusta mucho porque es emocionante. Trabaja en un teatro. *My father works as a cook and he really likes his job because it is interesting. He works in a school.*

b. Mi tía trabaja como mujer de negocios en una oficina. Le gusta pero es duro. *My aunt works as a business woman in a hair salon. She hates it but it's hard.*

c. Mi amigo Fran trabaja como enfermero. Trabaja en un hospital y le gusta su trabajo. *My enemy Fran works as a nurse. He lives in a hospital and likes his work.*

d. Mi tío Gianfranco es cocinero en un restaurante italiano y le encanta. *My uncle Gianfranco is a lawyer in an Italian restroom and he likes it.*

e. Mi madre Angela es contable y trabaja en una oficina. Odia su trabajo porque es aburrido y repetitivo. *My mother Angela is an actress and works in an office. She loves her work because it is boring and repetitive.*

3. Phrase-level translation En to Sp

a. my big brother

b. works as

c. a farmer

d. he likes

e. his job

f. because it's active

g. and fun

h. but it's tough

2. Translate into English

a. Mi tío trabaja de

b. Mi padre trabaja como

c. Amo de casa

d. Enfermera

e. Peluquero

f. Mecánico

g. Le encanta su trabajo

h. Trabaja en un taller

i. Trabaja en un teatro

j. Trabaja en un garaje

k. Es gratificante

l. Es duro pero divertido

4. Sentence-level translation En to Sp

a. My brother is a mechanic

b. My father is a business man

c. My uncle is a farmer and hates his job

d. My brother Darren works in a restaurant

e. At home I have a snake called Sally

f. At home I have a fun dog and a mean cat

g. My aunt is a nurse. She likes her job…

h. …because it is rewarding

i. My aunt works in a hospital

Unit 8. Saying what jobs people do: WRITING

1. Split sentences

Mi hermano tiene	estimulante
Mi tía es	como abogado
Mi primo trabaja	profesora
Le gusta	un restaurante
Porque es	empresa
Trabaja en	su trabajo
Trabaja en una	un pato negro

2. Rewrite the sentences in the correct order

a. Le su trabajo gusta mucho

b. Trabaja en una contable de oficina

c. Es y le ama de casa gusta

d. como tío granjero Mi trabaja

e. trabaja Mi hermano un teatro en

f. Mi odia su abuelo trabajo

g. Mi es médico amigo y en un trabaja hospital

3. Spot and correct the grammar and spelling note: in several cases a word is missing

a. Mi madre es amo de casa

b. Es una trabajo aburrido y difícil

c. Mi hermana trabaja como peluquero

d. Ella odia su trabajo porque es dura y repetitivo

e. Trabaja en una hospital en el ciudad

f. Le gusto mucho su trabajo porque es fácil

g. Mi parde odio su trabaja

h. Le gusta su trabajo porque es gratificantes

4. Anagrams

a. Micédo

b. Gratantifice

c. Ritipetevo

d. eL stGua

e. janaGr

f. taurResante

g. Psorrofe

6. Describe this person in Spanish in the 3rd person:

Name: Magdalena

Hair: Blond + green eyes

Physique: Tall and slim

Personality: Hard-working

Job: Nurse

Opinion: Likes her job a lot

Reason: Stressful but rewarding

5. Guided writing – write 3 short paragraphs describing the people below using the details in the box in 1st person

Person	Relation	Job	Like/ Dislike	Reason
Jorge	My dad	Mechanic	Loves	Active and interesting
Luciano	My brother	Lawyer	Hates	Boring and repetitive
Marta	My aunt	Farmer	Likes	Tough but fun

Grammar Time 4: The present indicative of
"Trabajar" and other AR verbs

yo	**trabajo** *I work*		**abogado/a** *lawyer*
tú	**trabajas** *you work*		**ama de casa** *house- wife*
			amo de casa *house-husband*
él			**cocinero/a** *chef*
mi hermano	**trabaja** *he works*		**contable** *accountant*
mi padre			**dependiente/a** *shop assistant*
ella		**como**	**enfermero/a** *nurse*
mi hermana	**trabaja** *she works*		**fontanero/a** *plumber*
mi madre		**(as)**	**granjero/a** *farmer*
nosotros			**hombre de negocios** *business man*
mi padre y yo	**trabajamos** *we work*		**ingeniero/a** *engineer*
vosotros	**trabajáis** *you guys work*		**mecánico/a** *mechanic*
vosotras	**trabajáis** *you ladies work*		**médico/a** *doctor*
ellos, ellas			**mujer de negocios** *businesswoman*
mis hermanos	**trabajan** *they work*		**peluquero/a** *hairdresser*
mis hermanas			**profesor/a** *teacher*

Drills

1. Match up

Trabaja	I work
Trabajo	You work
Trabajan	S/he works
Trabajáis	We work
Trabajamos	You guys work
Trabajas	They work

2. Translate into English

a. Trabajo de vez en cuando

b. Mis padres trabajan mucho

c. Mi hermano y yo no trabajamos

d. Ella no trabaja nunca

e. ¿Trabajas como bombero?

f. ¿Vosotros trabajáis en una tienda?

3. Complete with the correct option

a. Mi hermano _____ como peluquero

b. Mis padres no _____

c. Mi hermana y yo no _____

d. Mi novia _____ como azafata

e. Mis abuelos no _____

f. (vosotros) ¿ _____ como policías?

g. ¿Porque (tú) no _____?

h. (yo) No _____ todavía

trabajamos	trabaja	trabajan	trabajas
trabajan	trabaja	trabajáis	trabajo

 **THE LANGUAGE GYM**

4. Cross out the wrong option

	A	B
Mis padres	trabajan	trabajáis
Mi hermano	trabajas	trabaja
Mi padre	trabaja	trabajo
Mis tíos	trabajáis	trabajan
Mis tías	trabajan	trabajamos
Tú y yo	trabajamos	trabajáis
Nosotras	trabajamos	trabajan
Vosotros	trabaja	trabajáis
Mis primos	trabajan	trabajáis
Yo y ella	trabajamos	trabajan

5. Complete the verbs

a. Mi hermano y yo no trabaj __ __ __ __

b. Mis padres no trabaj __ __

c. Mi padre trabaj __ como abogado

d. Mis hermanos no trabaj __ __

e. Tú trabaj __ __ mucho

f. Mi madre trabaj __ en casa

g. Mis tíos trabaj __ __ como cocineros

h. Mi novia trabaj __ en una tienda de moda

i. ¡Vosotros no trabaj __ __ __ nunca!

6. Complete with the correct form of TRABAJAR

a. Mis padres _____ como obreros *My parents work as workers*

b. Mi madre _____ de profesora *My mother works as a teacher*

c. Mis padres _____ como contables *My parents work as accountants*

d. Mi padre _____ como periodista *My father works as a journalist*

e. Mi hermano no _____ *My brother doesn't work*

f. Mis hermanas no _____ tampoco *My sisters don't work either*

g. Mi tío _____ de bombero *My uncle works as a fireman*

h. Mis primos y yo no _____ *My cousins and I don't work*

i. (yo) _____ en un restaurante *I work in a restaurant*

j. Mi novia _____ en una tienda de ropa *My girlfriend works in a clothing store*

k. ¿Dónde_____ ? *Where do you work?*

Verbs like TRABAJAR

Adorar: to love

Cenar: to have dinner

Desayunar: to eat for breakfast

Escuchar: to listen to

Estudiar: to study

Hablar: to speak

Practicar: to practise

Tocar: to play (an instrument)

Tomar: to take, eat

7. Complete the sentences using the correct form of the verbs in the grey box on the left

a. Ador__ a mis abuelos *I love my grandparents*

b. Desayun__ cereales *He has cereals for breakfast*

c. Practic_____ el esquí *We practise skiing*

d. ¿Habl___ español? *Do you speak Spanish?*

e. ¿Dónde cen___ ? *Where do you have dinner?*

f. ¿Toc_____ la guitarra? *Do you guys play the guitar?*

g. Escuch___ música rock *I listen to rock music*

h. Nunca tom___ café *I never have coffee*

Grammar Time 5: SER (Part 2)
(Present indicative of "Ser" and jobs)

Present Indicative of 'Ser'		Jobs (nouns)	
		Singular	**Plural**
MASCULINE			
yo	**soy** *I am*	actor	actores
tú	**eres** *you are*	abogado	abogados
		amo de casa	amos de casa
él		cocinero	cocineros
mi hermano	**es** *he is*	contable	contables
mi padre		dependiente	dependientes
nosotros	**somos** *we are*	enfermero	enfermeros
mi padre y yo		granjero	granjeros
		ingeniero	ingenieros
vosotros	**sois** *you guys are*	mecánico	mecánicos
		médico	médicos
ellos,		peluquero	peluqueros
mis hermanos	**son** *they are*	profesor	profesores
mis padres			
FEMININE			
yo	**soy** *I am*	actriz	actrices
tú	**eres** *are*	abogada	abogadas
		ama de casa	amas de casa
ella		cocinera	cocineras
mi hermana	**es** *she is*	contable	contables
mi madre		dependienta	dependientas
nosotras	**somos** *we are*	enfermera	enfermeras
mi madre y yo		granjera	granjeras
		ingeniera	ingenieras
vosotras	**sois** *you ladies are*	mecánica	mecánicas
		médica	médicas
ellas		peluquera	peluqueras
mis hermanas	**son** *they are*	profesora	profesoras
mis tías			

Drills

1. Match

Soy	She/he is
Somos	You are
Son	We are
Eres	I am
Es	They are
Sois	You guys are

2. Complete with the missing forms of SER

a. Mi madre y yo _____ médicas

b. Mis hermanos _____ obreros

c. Mi hermana _____ enfermera

d. Mis padres y yo _____ jardineros

e. (tú) ¿_____ abogado?

f. (yo) _____ bombero

g. (ellos) No _____ policías

h. (vosotras) ¿_____ modelos?

i. (vosotros) _____ actores, ¿verdad?

j. Mis tíos _____ cantantes famosos

3. Translate into English

a. Somos peluqueros

b. Son policías

c. ¿Eres bombero?

d. María es modelo

e. Son obreros en una obra *(building site)*

f. Soy policía

g. ¿Sois enfermeras?

h. Somos médicos

i. Mi padre y yo somos actores

j. ¿Sois profesores?

k. Soy fontanero

4. Translate into Spanish (easier)

a. My father is a doctor

b. My parents are policemen

c. My uncle is a lawyer

d. I am a teacher

e. My cousins are mechanics

f. My aunt is a singer

g. My friend Valentino is an actor

5. Translate into Spanish (harder)

a. My brother is tall and handsome. He is an actor.

b. My older sister is very intelligent and hard-working. She is a scientist.

c. My younger brother is very sporty and active. He is a gym instructor.

d. My mother is very strong and hard-working. She is a doctor.

e. My father is very patient, calm and organized. He is an accountant.

UNIT 9
Comparing people's appearance and personality

In this unit will learn how to say in Spanish:

- More/less ... than
- As ... as
- New adjectives to describe people

You will revisit the following:

- Family members
- Pets
- Describing animals' appearance and character

UNIT 9
Comparing people

Él		**aburrido/a** *boring*		él
Ella		**alto/a** *tall*		ella
Mi abuela		**amable** *kind*		mi abuela
Mi abuelo		**antipático/a** *unfriendly*		mi abuelo
Mi amiga <u>Ana</u>		**bajo/a** *short*		mi amiga <u>Ana</u>
Mi amigo <u>Paco</u>	**más** more	**cariñoso/a** *affectionate*		mi amigo <u>Paco</u>
Mi gato		**débil** *weak*		mi gato
Mi hermana		**delgado/a** *slim*		mi hermana
Mi hermano		**deportista** *sporty*		mi hermano
Mi hijo	**es** is	**divertido/a** *fun*	**que** than	mi hijo
Mi hija		**feo/a** *ugly*		mi hija
Mi madre		**fuerte** *strong*		mi madre
Mi mejor amiga		**gordo/a** *fat*		mi mejor amiga
Mi mejor amigo		**guapo/a** *good-looking*		mi mejor amigo
Mi padre	**menos** less	**hablador(a)** *talkative*		nosotros *us*
Mi pato		**inteligente** *intelligent*		mi padre
Mi perro		**joven** *young*		mis padres
Mi prima		**perezoso/a** *lazy*		mi pato
Mi primo		**ruidoso/a** *noisy*		mi perro
Mi tortuga	**son** are	**serio/a** *serious*	**como** as	mi prima
Mi tía		**simpático/a** *nice*		mi primo
Mi tío		**trabajador(a)** *hard-working*		mi tortuga
Mis abuelos	**tan** as			mi tía
Mis hermanas		**tranquilo/a** *relaxed*		mi tío
Mis hermanos		**tonto/a** *stupid*		mis abuelos
Mi novio *(bf)*		**viejo/a** *old*		mis hermanas
Mi novia *(gf)*				mis hermanos
Mis padres				mis primos
Mis tíos				mis tíos
				yo

Author's note: *Add an 'S' at the end of your adjectives for plurals (when describing more than one person). E.g. Mis padres son más TRANQUILOS que mis tíos.*

Unit 9. Comparing people : VOCABULARY BUILDING

1. Complete with the missing word

a. Mi padre es más alto _____ mi hermano mayor — *My father is taller than my older brother*

b. Mi madre es _____ habladora que mi _____ — *My mother is less talkative than my aunt*

c. Mi _____ es más bajo que _____ padre — *My grandfather is shorter than my dad*

d. Mis primos son _____ perezosos que _____ — *My cousins are lazier than us*

e. Mi perro _____ más _____ que mi _____ — *My dog is more noisy than my cat*

f. Mi tía es _____ guapa que _____ madre — *My aunt is less pretty than my mother*

g. Mi _____ es más _____ que yo — *My bro is more hard-working than me*

h. Mis padres _____ más _____ que mis tíos — *My parents are more kind than my uncles*

i. Mi hermano menor es _____ alto _____ yo — *My younger brother is as tall as me*

2. Translate into English

a. mis primos

b. más

c. mi tío

d. mis abuelos

e. mi hermana

f. mi mejor amigo

g. trabajador

h. mi amiga

i. alto

j. viejo

k. terco

l. perezoso

3. Match Spanish and English

trabajador	strong
guapo	stupid
amable	sporty
fuerte	good-looking
deportista	old
viejo	hard-working
tonto	kind

4. Spot and correct any English translation mistakes

a. Es más alto que yo — *He is taller than you*

b. Es tan guapo como yo — *He is as funny as me*

c. Es más tranquila que yo — *She is stronger than me*

d. Soy menos gordo que él — *I am more fat than him*

e. Son menos bajos que nosotros — *They are shorter than us*

f. Soy tan viejo como él — *She is as old as him*

g. Es más deportista que yo — *You are more sporty than me*

5. Complete with a suitable word

a. Mi madre es _____ alta _____ yo

b. ____ padre _____ más joven que mi tío

c. Mis padres son _____ altos como _____ abuelos

d. _____ hermanos _____ más deportistas que mis primos

e. Mi _____ es menos ruidoso _____ mi pato

f. Mis abuelos _____ tan cariñosos _____ mis padres

g. Mi novia es _____ guapa que _____ tortuga

h. Mi tío no _____ tan fuerte _____ mi _____

6. Match the opposites

guapo	bajo
trabajador	aburrido
joven	feo
alto	gordo
divertido	menos
débil	perezoso
más	viejo
delgado	fuerte

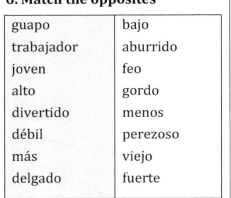

THE LANGUAGE GYM

Unit 9. Comparing people : READING

Me llamo Jorge. Tengo veinte años y vivo en Buenos Aires. En mi familia somos cinco personas: mis padres y mis dos hermanos, Felipe y Ale. Felipe es más alto, guapo y fuerte que Ale, pero Ale es más amable, inteligente y trabajador que Felipe.

Mis padres se llaman Antonio y Nina. Ambos son muy amables, pero mi padre es más estricto que mi madre. Además, mi madre es más paciente y menos terca que mi padre. ¡Yo soy tan terco como mi padre!

En casa tenemos dos mascotas: una tortuga y un pato. Ambos son muy simpáticos, pero mi pato es más ruidoso. Tan ruidoso como yo...

Me llamo José García. Tengo quince años y vivo en Ceuta. En mi familia somos cinco personas: mis padres y mis dos hermanos, Rubén y Pedro. Rubén es más delgado y deportista que Pedro, pero Pedro es más alto y fuerte.

Mis padres se llaman Carmen y Antonio. Prefiero a mi padre porque es menos estricto que mi madre. Además, mi madre es más terca que mi padre. ¡Yo soy tan terco como ella! En casa tenemos dos mascotas: un loro y una cobaya. Ambos son muy simpáticos, pero mi loro es mucho más hablador. Tan hablador como yo...

Me llamo Victoria. Tengo veinte años y vivo en Toledo con mis padres y mis dos hermanas, Marina y Verónica. Marina es más hermosa que Verónica, pero Verónica es más simpática.

Mis padres son muy cariñosos y amables, pero mi padre es más divertido que mi madre. Además, mi padre es más gracioso que mi madre. ¡Yo soy tan gracioso como mi padre!

En casa tenemos dos mascotas: un perro y un conejo. Ambos son muy gordos, pero mi perro es más perezoso. Tan perezoso como yo...

1. Find the Spanish for the following in Jorge's text

a. I live in:

b. My parents:

c. Good-looking:

d. Hard-working:

e. Less stubborn:

f. More patient:

g. But:

h. My duck:

i. Two pets:

j. Very kind:

k. As stubborn as:

2. Complete the statements below based on Victoria's text

a. I am _____ years old

b. Marina is more _____ than Verónica

c. Verónica is more _____

d. My parents are very _____ and _____

e. I am as _____ as my father

f. We have _____ pets: a _____ and a _____

3. Correct any of the statements below (about José Garcia's text) which are incorrect

a. José tiene tres mascotas

b. Rubén es menos gordo que Pedro

c. Rubén es más débil que Pedro

d. José es tan hablador como su cobaya

e. José prefiere a su madre

f. José es más terco que su madre

4. Answer the questions on the three texts above

a. Where does José live?

b. Who is stricter, his mother or his father?

c. Who is as talkative as their parrot?

d. Who is as chatty as their duck?

e. Who has a stubborn father?

f. Who has a rabbit?

g. Who has a guinea pig?

h. Which one of José's brothers is sportier?

i. What are the differences between Jorge's brothers?

Unit 9. Comparing people: TRANSLATION/WRITING

1. Translate into English

a. Alto

b. Delgado

c. Bajo

d. Gordo

e. Inteligente

f. Terco

g. Tonto

h. Guapo

i. Feo

j. Más...que

k. Menos...que

l. Fuerte

m. Débil

n. Tan...como...

2. Gapped sentences

a. Mi _____ es _____ alta _____ mi tía

My mother is taller than my aunt

b. _____ padre _____ más _____ que mi hermano mayor

My father is stronger than my older brother

c. Mis _____ son menos _____ que nosotros

My cousins are less sporty than us

d. _____ hermano es _____ tonto que _____

My brother is more stupid than me

e. Mi madre _____ _____ amable _____ mi padre

My mother is as kind as my father

f. Mi _____ es _____ trabajadora que _____

My sister is more hard-working than us

g. Mi _____ es menos _____ _____ yo

My girlfriend is less serious than me

h. Mi _____ es _____ terco _____ mi abuela

My grandfather is more stubborn than my grandmother

3. Phrase-level translation En to Sp

a. My mother is

b. Taller than

c. As slim as

d. Less stubborn than

e. I am shorter than

f. My parents are

g. My cousins are

h. As fat as

i. They are as strong as

j. My grandparents are

k. I am as lazy as

4. Sentence-level translation En to Sp

a. My older sister is taller than my younger sister.

b. My father is as stubborn as my mother.

c. My girlfriend is more hard-working than me.

d. I am less intelligent than my brother.

e. My best friend is stronger and sportier than me.

f. My boyfriend is better-looking than me.

g. My cousins are uglier than us.

h. My duck is noisier than my dog.

i. My cat is more fun than my turtle.

j. My rabbit is less fat than my guinea pig.

THE LANGUAGE GYM

Revision Quickie 2 : Family, Pets and Jobs

1. Match

Obrero	Doctor
Abogado	Waiter
Enfermero	Journalist
Camarero	Nurse
Periodista	IT worker
Médico	Worker
Azafata	Air hostess
Bombero	Lawyer
Informático	Firefighter

2. Sort the words listed below in the categories in the table

a. obrero; b. alto; c. fontanero; d. gracioso; e. bajo; f. primo;
g. profesora; h. enfermero; i. tío; j. padre ; k. azul; l. gordo; m. guapo;
n. bombero; o. madre; p. hermano; q. conejo; r. castaño; s. pato; t. gato

Descripciones	Animales	Trabajos	Familia

3. Complete with the missing adjectives

a. Mi padre es _____ *fat*

b. Mi madre es _____ *tall*

c. Mi hermano es _____ *short*

d. Mi novia es _____ *pretty*

e. Mi primo es _____ *annoying*

f. Mi profe de inglés es _____ *boring*

5. Match the opposites

Alto	Trabajador
Guapo	Estúpido
Gordo	Bajo
Perezoso	Silencioso
Inteligente	Feo
Ruidoso	Impaciente
Malo	Delgado
Paciente	Bueno

6. Complete the numbers below

a. Cato_ _ _   14

b. Cuare_ _ _ _   40

c. Sese_ _ _   60

d. Cincu_ _ _ _   50

e. Seten_ _   70

f. Nove_ _ _   90

4. Complete with the missing nouns

a. Mi padre trabaja como _____ *lawyer*

b. Mi madre es _____ *nurse*

c. Mi mejor amigo es _____ *journalist*

d. Mi hermana es _____ *air hostess*

e. Mi primo es _____ *student*

f. Yo trabajo como _____ *doctor*

g. Marta es _____ *sales assistant*

h. Mi abuela es _____ *singer*

7. Complete with the correct verb

a. Mi madre ___ alta   *My mother is tall*

b. _____ el pelo negro *I have black hair*

c. _____ como fontanero *I work as a plumber*

d. Mi padre _____ cuarenta años *My father is 40*

e. ¿Cuántas personas _____ en tu familia?
How many people are there in your family?

f. Mis hermanos _____ altos *My brothers are tall*

g. Mi hermano no _____
My brother doesn't work

h. Mi novia ___ _____ Gabi
My girlfriend is called Gabi

THE LANGUAGE GYM

UNIT 10
Saying what's in my school bag / classroom/ describing colour

Grammar Time: Tener & Agreements

In this unit will learn how to say:

- What objects you have is in your schoolbag/pencil case/classroom
- Words for classroom equipment
- What you have and don't have

You will revisit the following:
- Colours
- How adjectives agree in gender and number with nouns
- Introducing yourself (e.g. name, age, town, country)
- Pets

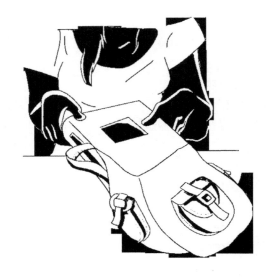

UNIT 10.
Saying what's in my school bag/ classroom/describing colour

En mi mochila *in my schoolbag*		En mi clase *in my class*
Hay / No hay *There is / There isn't*	**un bolígrafo** *a pen*	negr**o**
	un cuaderno *an exercise book*	blanc**o**
	un diccionario *a dictionary*	amarill**o**
	un estuche *a pencil case*	
	un lápiz *a pencil*	roj**o**
	un libro *a book*	azul
Tengo / No tengo *I have / I don't have*	**un ordenador** *a computer*	verde
	un papel *a paper*	gris
	un pegamento *a gluestick*	
	un rotulador *a felt tip pen*	rosa
	un sacapuntas *a pencil sharpener*	naranja
No me hace falta *I don't need*	**unos bolígrafos** *some pens*	amarillo**s**
	unos lápices *some pencils*	marron**es**
	unos rotuladores *some felt tip pens*	naranja**s**
Mi amigo Paco tiene *My friend Paco has*	**una agenda** *a planner*	negr**a**
	una calculadora *a calculator*	blanc**a**
	una goma *a rubber*	amarill**a**
	una mesa *a table*	roj**a**
	una pizarra *a whiteboard*	azul
Mi amigo Paco no tiene *My friend Paco does not have*	**una pluma** *a fountain pen*	gris
	una regla *a ruler*	rosa
	una silla *a chair*	naranja
	tijeras *scissors*	amarilla**s**

Unit 10. Saying what's in my school bag: VOCABULARY BUILDING

1. Complete with the missing word

a. Tengo un _____   *I have an exercise book*

b. Me hace falta una _____   *I need an eraser*

c. No tengo ___ bolígrafo   *I don't have a pen*

d. Mi amigo _____un papel   *My friend has a paper*

e. Tengo ____ calculadora   *I have a calculator*

f. Me hace falta una _____   *I need a chair*

g. No tengo una _____   *I don't have a ruler*

h. Mi amigo tiene _____   *My friend has scissors*

2. Match up

una goma	a pencil
un lápiz	a planner
una agenda	I have a...
una silla	a sharpener
tengo un	a pen
me hace falta	I don't have a
no tengo un	a chair
un sacapuntas	an eraser
un bolígrafo	I need a

3. Translate into English

a. Tengo una goma

b. Mi amigo tiene una agenda

c. No tengo un cuaderno

d. Tengo un lápiz

e. No tengo un sacapuntas

f. Me hace falta un rotulador

g. Hay un ordenador

h. No tengo un rotulador

4. Add the missing letter

a. Un sacapun__as

b. Una g_ma

c. Me hace f_lta

d. No ten_o

e. Una __genda

f. Mi ami__o

g. No t_ene

h. Una pi__arra

5. Anagrams

a. páLices Lápices

b. chEestu

c. jaraNan

d. Blcano

e. erTijas

f. choMila

g. megaPento

h. rdVee

6. Broken words

a. E__ m___ m_____ t_____ u__ e_____
In my bag I have a pencil case

b. E__ m___ e_____ t_____ u____ l_____
In my pencil case I have some pencils

c. N__ t_____ u____ g_____   *I don't have an eraser*

d. M__ h_____ f_____ u____ r_____   *I need a ruler*

e. H____ u_____ p_____   *There is a whiteboard*

f. T_____ u___ b_____ a_____   *I have some blue pens*

g. M___ h_____ f_____ u__ r_____   *I need a felt tip pen*

7. Complete with a suitable word

a. Tengo un _____

b. Me hace _____ un lápiz

c. Me gusta el color _____

d. _____ un ordenador

e. Un lápiz _____

f. Una _____ roja

g. Mi _____ tiene un estuche

h. ___ tengo una regla

i. Mi amigo no _____ un rotulador

j. Unos lápices _____

k. Hay _____ pizarra

Unit 10. Saying what's in my school bag: READING

Me llamo Renata. Tengo doce años y vivo en Roma, en Italia. En mi familia hay cuatro personas. Tengo un gato blanco. En mi mochila tengo muchas cosas. Tengo un lápiz rojo, un bolígrafo amarillo, una regla roja y una goma blanca. La goma es mi favorita. Mi amiga Lucía solo tiene una cosa en su estuche, un lápiz. ¡Pero en su casa tiene un caballo gris!

Me llamo Andrea. Tengo quince años y vivo en París, en Francia. En mi familia hay tres personas. Tengo una cobaya muy divertida. En mi clase hay muchas cosas. Hay una pizarra, un ordenador y treinta mesas. Mi clase es muy grande. Tengo un lápiz azul, un rotulador amarillo, una regla nueva y una goma. Mi amigo Martín tiene lápices de todos los colores.

Me llamo Lucas. Tengo dieciocho años y vivo en Cádiz, en España. En mi familia hay cinco personas. Mi hermano se llama Andy. En mi clase hay una pizarra, y veinte mesas. También hay veinte sillas. Una para cada persona. Mi clase es bonita y mi profesor es muy divertido. Pero, no tengo un lápiz, ni un bolígrafo, ni una regla, ni una goma. No tengo nada. Me hace falta todo, básicamente. En casa tengo una rata blanca muy graciosa.

Me llamo Emiliano. Tengo once años y vivo en México D.F., la capital de México. En mi familia hay cuatro personas. Me encanta mi madre pero no me gusta mi padre. Siempre es muy antipático. Él es abogado. En mi clase no hay muchas cosas. No hay ni una pizarra ni un ordenador. Hay veintiocho mesas, pero solo hay veintisiete sillas. ¡Es un problema! Tengo un lápiz, una calculadora y una agenda.

1. Find the Spanish in Renata's text

a. I am 12

b. I live in Rome

c. There are 4 people

d. A white cat

e. A red pencil

f. A yellow pen

g. It is my favourite

h. Only has one thing

i. In her house

j. A grey horse

2. Find Someone Who...

a. ...has a blue pencil

b. ...has most tables in their class

c. ...has a class with one student always standing

d. ...has no school equipment

e. ...has a big pet

f. ...doesn't like their dad

3. Answer the following questions about Lucas' text

a. Where does Lucas live?

b. Who is Andy?

c. How many tables and chairs are there in his class?

d. How does he describe his class?

e. What school equipment does he have?

f. What pet does he have?

g. How does he describe his pet?

5. Fill in the blanks about José Luis

Me l_____ José Luis. Tengo ocho a_____ y v_____ en Elche, en España. En mi familia h_____ cuatro personas. En mi c_____ hay muchas cosas, como u___ ordenador y una p_____. En mi e_____ tengo un l_____, un bolígrafo a_____ y una g_____. Mi amig___ tiene muchos lá_____ pero no tiene una g_____. Me gusta mucho mi pro_____ porque es muy sim_____. ¡En casa tengo _____ serpiente verde!

4. Fill in the table below

Name	Renata	Andrea
Age		
City		
Items in pencil case		

Unit 10. Saying what's in my school bag: TRANSLATION

1. Faulty translation: spot and correct *in the English* any translation mistakes you find below

a. En mi clase hay dos pizarras y un ordenador. No me gusta mi profesor *In my class there is a whiteboard and a computer. I like my teacher.*

b. No tengo muchas cosas en mi estuche. Tengo un lápiz rosa pero no tengo una regla *I have many things in my pencil case. I have a red pencil but I don't have an eraser.*

c. My amigo Emilio tiene cuatro personas en su familia. Necesita un rotulador negro y una agenda *My friend Emilio has five people in his family. He needs a black pen and a diary.*

d. Me hace falta un sacapuntas y un pegamento . No tengo una regla o un bolígrafo. ¡Me encanta mi profesor! *I need paper and a rubber. I don't have a ruler or a pencil. I hate my teacher!*

e. En mi clase hay treinta mesas y treinta sillas. Me hace falta una agenda pero sí tengo un diccionario *In my class there are thirty cats and thirty chairs. I need a calculator but I have a dictionary.*

2. Translate into English

a. Me hace falta un

b. Tengo un lápiz negro

c. Tengo un bolígrafo azul

d. Una regla verde

e. Tengo un perro en casa

f. Mi amigo tiene un libro

g. Mi padre trabaja como

h. Me gusta mi profesor

i. Unos lápices amarillos

j. Una pizarra grande

k. Tengo muchas cosas

l. No tengo un sacapuntas

m. Me hace falta un diccionario

3. Phrase-level translation En to Sp

a. A red book

b. A black calculator

c. I don't have

d. I need a...

e. I like

f. There are...

g. I have

h. My friend has...

4. Sentence-level translation En to Sp

a. There are 20 tables

b. There is a whiteboard

c. My teacher is nice

d. I have some blue pens

e. I have some orange pencils

f. I need an eraser and a sharpener

g. I need a chair and a book

h. My class is very big and pretty

i. My father is a teacher

Unit 10. Saying what's in my school bag: WRITING

1. Split sentences

Tengo una	tiene una pluma
Me hace	gusta mi tío
Mi clase	falta un lápiz
Hay treinta	calculadora
Mi amigo no	es grande
No me	bolígrafo
Tengo un	mesas

2. Rewrite the sentences in the correct order

a. Me falta hace calculadora una

b. Tengo una regla roja un lápiz y negro

c. Mi muy grande clase es

d. Mi amigo libro blanco tiene un

e. No azul tengo una agenda

f. En mi tortuga verde tengo una casa

g. Mi es médico padre y en un trabaja hospital

3. Spot and correct the grammar and spelling note: in several cases a word is missing

a. En mi clase hay veinte mesa.

b. Tengo un calculadora negra.

c. En mi estuche yo tiene muchas cosas.

d. Mi amigo no tengo nada en su estuches.

e. Mi hace falta un lápiz y un goma.

f. Mi amigo Fernando tiene lápiz de todos los color.

g. Mi madre es mecánico y trabaja en una garaje.

h. Soy alto y fuerte. Tengo el pelo rubia y los ojos azul.

4. Anagrams

a. tuesche

b. pirazar

c. borlífoga

d. smase

e. rulotador

f. sacatapuns

g. prsorofe

5. Guided writing – write 4 short paragraphs describing the people below using the details in the box (in 1st person)

Person	Lives	Has	Hasn't	Needs
Natalia	Madrid	Exercise book	Pen	Diary
Iker	Pamplona	Ruler	Pencil	A paper
Julieta	Valencia	Felt tip	Sharpener	A gluestick

6. Describe this person in Spanish:

Name: Diego

Pet: A black horse

Hair: brown + blue eyes

School equipment: has pen, pencil, ruler, eraser

Does not have: sharpener, paper, chair

Favourite colour: blue

Grammar Time 6: TENER (Part 3) + AGREEMENTS
Present indicative of "Tener" (to have) and agreement training

Tengo *I have* **Tienes** *you have* **Tiene** *he/she has* **Tenemos** *we have* **Tenéis** *you guys have* **Tienen** *they have*	**No tengo** *I don't have* **No tienes** *you don't have* **No tiene** *he/she doesn't have* **No tenemos** *we don't have* **No tenéis** *you guys don't have* **No tienen** *they don'thave*
un bolígrafo una calculadora un cuaderno un diccionario un estuche un lápiz un libro un ordenador un rotulador	doce años trece años catorce años quince años dieciséis años diecisiete años dieciocho años diecinueve años veinte años
clase de arte a las ocho clase de ciencias a las nueve clase de español a las diez clase de francés a las once clase de geografía a las doce clase de historia a la una clase de matemáticas a las dos clase de educación física a las tres profesores muy buenos profesores muy malos	un caballo un conejo un gato un hámster un loro un pájaro un pato un perro un pez un ratón
un hermano, una hermana un hijo, una hija un tío, una tía un novio, una novia	dos abuelos, dos abuelas dos hermanos, dos hermanas dos primos, dos primas

Present indicative of "Tener" + Agreements: Verb drills (1)

1. Match up

Tengo	We have
Tenemos	I have
Tienes	They have
Tiene	You have
Tenéis	He/she has
Tienen	You guys have

2. Complete with the missing word (pets/family members)

a. No _____ mascotas   *I don't have pets*

b. _____ un gato gris   *We have a grey cat*

c. _____ dos tortugas   *They have two turtles*

d. ¿_____ hermanos?   *Do you have siblings?*

e. ¿_____ mascotas?   *Do you guys have pets?*

f. Mi hermano _____ una cobaya   *My brother has a guinea pig*

g. Mi primo no _____ mascotas   *My cousin doesn't have pets*

h. Mis primos no _____ mascotas   *My cousins have no pets*

3. Complete with the present indicative form of "tener"

yo _____

tú _____

él, ella _____

nosotros _____

vosotros _____

ellos, ellas _____

4. Add in the correct verb ending

a. Mi primo no tien____ mascotas

b. Mis tíos tien_____ dos perros

c. Ahora (yo) ten_____ clase de historia

d. A las doce (nosotros) ten_____ geografía

e. Mi hermano tien_____ diez años

f. Mis padres tien_____ cuarenta años

g. Mi padre tien____ el pelo blanco

h. Mis hermanas tiene_____ el pelo pelirrojo

5. Complete with the missing form of "tener"

a. Mi padre _____ cuarenta años

b. Mi madre _____ treinta y dos años

c. Mis padres _____ los ojos azules, pero yo _____ los ojos negros

d. Mi tío Mario no _____ pelo

e. (tú) ¿_____ hermanos?

f. (vosotras) _____ el pelo muy hermoso

g. (yo) No _____ mascotas, pero mi hermano _____ una cobaya

6. Translate into Spanish

a. My father has blue eyes

b. I don't have pets

c. I don't have a pen

d. In my pencil case I have a ruler

e. Do you have any felt-tip pens?

f. I have a dog at home

g. My mother is 40

h. My father is 38

i. Do you guys have history today?

j. How old are you?

Present indicative of "Tener" + Agreements
Verb drills (2)

7. Translate the pronoun <u>and</u> verb into Spanish as shown in the example

I have: **(Yo) tengo**

You have: (   )

She has: (   )

He has: (   )

We have: (   )

You guys have: (   )

They (f) have: (   )

They (m) have: (   )

8. Translate into Spanish. Topic: Pets and colours

a. We have a blue parrot

b. I have two green turtles

c. My brother has a white guinea pig

d. My uncles have a black horse

e. My sister has a red and black spider

f. We don't have pets at home

g. Do you have pets at home?

9. Translate into Spanish. Topic: family members

a. I don't have brothers

b. We have two grandparents

c. My mother has no sisters

d. Do you have any brothers or sisters?

e. Do you guys have cousins?

f. I don't have any brothers

10. Translate into Spanish. Topic: Age

a. They are fifteen years old

b. We are fourteen years old

c. I am sixteen years old

d. You guys are twelve years old

e. How old are you?

f. My mother is forty

11. Translate into Spanish. Topic: Hair and eyes

a. I have black hair

b. We have blue eyes

c. She has curly hair

d. My mother has blond hair

e. Do you have grey eyes ?

f. They have green eyes

g. My brother has brown eyes

h. We have no hair

j. You guys have beautiful eyes

k. My parents have red hair

l. You have no hair

m. My sister has very long hair

Grammar Time 7: Agreements (Part 1)

1. Complete the table

English	Español
Yellow	
	Rosa, Rosado
	Gris
Green	
Red	
	Morado
	Naranja
Black	
	Blanco
Blue	

2. Translate into English

a. Un lápiz amarillo:

b. Un estuche negro:

c. Dos cuadernos rosados:

d. Unos rotuladores rojos:

e. Una pluma azul:

f. Dos plumas azules:

g. Una mochila naranja:

h. Un sacapuntas gris:

i. Una pluma roja:

j. Una mochila amarilla y roja:

3. Provide the feminine version of each adjective in the table

Masculino	Femenino
amarillo	
verde	
azul	
rojo	
blanco	
negro	
naranja	

4. Complete with the missing adjective

a. Tengo una mochila _____ *I have a red schoolbag*

b. Tengo un bolígrafo _____ *I have a black pen*

c. Tengo una pluma _____ *I have a blue fountain pen*

d. Tengo una regla _____ *I have a yellow ruler*

e. Tengo una hoja _____ *I have a white sheet of paper*

f. Tengo dos tijeras _____ *I have two red scissors*

g. Tengo unos rotuladores _____ *I have some blue markers*

h. Tengo una mochila _____ *I have a black schoolbag*

5. Translate into Spanish

a. a red fountain pen

b. a black ruler

c. a green schoolbag

d. a yellow pencil case

e. two green rulers

f. two blue scissors

g. two pink exercise books

6. Translate into Spanish

a. I have a red pen and a blue fountain pen

b. Felipe has a green schoolbag

c. Do you have a white pencil case?

d. Do you guys have any red markers?

e. I have a pink sheet of paper

f. We have a yellow schoolbag

g. He has a black and white ruler

UNIT 11 (Part 1)
Talking about food:
Likes / Dislikes / Reasons

Grammar Time: Comer /Beber

In this unit will learn how to say:

- What food you like/dislike and to what extent
- Why you like/dislike it (old and new expressions)
- New adjectives
- The full conjugation of 'comer' *to eat* and 'beber' *to drink*

You will revisit the following
- Time markers
- Providing a justification

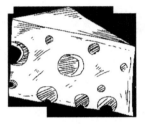

UNIT 11: Talking about food
Likes/ Dislikes / Reasons - Part 1

Singular

Me encanta *I love* **Me gusta** *I like* **Me gusta mucho** *I like a lot* **Me gusta un poco** *I like a bit* **Prefiero** *I prefer* **No me gusta** *I don't like* **Odio** *I hate*	**el pan** *bread* **el pescado** *fish* **el pollo asado** *roast chicken* **el queso** *cheese* **el zumo de fruta** *fruit juice* **el arroz** *rice* **el café** *coffee* **el chocolate** *chocolate*	**porque es** *because* *it is*	**asqueroso** *disgusting* **delicioso** *delicious* **dulce** *sweet* **duro** *tough* **grasiento** *greasy* *** picante** *spicy* **rico en proteínas** *rich in protein* **sano** *healthy*
	el agua *water* **la ensalada verde *green salad* **la carne** *meat* **la fruta** *fruit* **la leche** *milk* **la miel** *honey*		**malsana** *unhealthy* **refrescante** *refreshing* **rica en proteínas** *rich in protein* **sabrosa** *tasty* **sana** *healthy*

Plural

Me encantan *I love* **Me gustan mucho** *I like a lot* **Me gustan** *I like* **Me gustan un poco** *I like a bit* **No me gustan** *I don't like* **Odio** *I hate* **Prefiero** *I prefer*	**los chocolates** *chocolates* **los huevos** *eggs* **los plátanos** *bananas* **los tomates** *tomatoes*	**porque son** *because* *they are*	**asquerosos** *disgusting* **deliciosos** *delicious* **dulces** *sweet* **duros** *tough* **malsanos** *unhealthy*
	las gambas *prawns* **las hamburguesas** *burgers* **las manzanas** *apples* **las naranjas** *oranges* **las verduras** *vegetables*		**grasientos** *oily, greasy* **refrescantes** *refreshing* **ricas en proteínas** *rich in protein* **sabrosas** *tasty* **sanas** *healthy*

Author's note:
* Adjectives ending in 'e' do not change from masculine to feminine.
** El agua is actually feminine but starts with "el" to avoid the double "a" sound.

Unit 11. Talking about food (Part 1): VOCABULARY BUILDING (Part 1)

1. Match up

Los plátanos	Eggs
Las fresas	Apples
La carne	Prawns
El pollo	Milk
El agua	Fruit
La leche	Water
Los huevos	Burgers
Las gambas	Chicken
Las hamburguesas	Meat
La fruta	Bananas
Las manzanas	Strawberries

2. Complete

a. Me gusta mucho el _____   *I like chicken a lot*

b. Me encantan las _____   *I love prawns*

c. Me gustan las _____   *I like strawberries*

d. Me encanta la _____   *I love milk*

e. Me encantan los _____   *I love bananas*

f. Me encanta el _____ mineral   *I love mineral water*

g. No me gustan los _____   *I don't like tomatoes*

h. Odio el _____   *I hate chicken*

i. Me encanta la _____   *I love fruit*

j. No me gustan los _____   *I don't like eggs*

3. Translate into English

a. Me gusta la fruta

b. Odio los huevos

c. Me encanta el pollo asado

d. Me gustan las hamburguesas

e. Odio la carne

f. Prefiero las naranjas

g. No me gustan los tomates

h. Odio la leche

4. Complete the words

a. Los hu_____

b. Los pl_____

c. La fr_____

d. Las verd_____

e. Las hamb_____

f. Las ga_____

g. Las man_____

h. El a_____

5. Fill the gaps with either 'me gust<u>a</u>' or 'me gust<u>an</u>' as per your own preference

a. No _____los huevos

b. _____el agua

c. _____el pollo

d. _____las hamburguesas

e. _____las verduras

f. _____la carne

g. _____la fruta

h. _____las gambas

i. _____la pasta

6. Translate into Spanish

a. I like eggs

b. I love oranges

c. I hate tomatoes

d. I don't like prawns

e. I love fruit

f. I don't like vegetables

g. I hate milk

Unit 11. Talking about food (Part 1): VOCABULARY BUILDING (Part 2)

1. Complete with the missing words. The initial letter of each word is given

a. Estos plátanos son a_____

These bananas are disgusting

b. Estas manzanas son d_____

These apples are delicious

c. Este pollo es muy p_____

This chicken is very spicy

d. No me gusta la c_____

I don't like meat

e. Este café es muy d_____

This coffee is very sweet

f. Las hamburguesas son m_____

Burgers are unhealthy

g. Las verduras son s_____

Vegetables are healthy

h. Me encanta la l_____   *I love milk*

2. Complete the table

Español	English
La leche	
	Roast chicken
El pescado	
Los huevos	
	Water
	Bread
Los cereales	
El pan tostado	
	Vegetables

3. Complete with 'me gusta' or 'me gustan' as appropriate

a. _____ las manzanas

b. _____la leche

c. No _____los cereales

d. _____el pan tostado

e. _____las verduras

f. No _____la pasta

g. _____el arroz

h. No _____el café

4. Broken words

a. N__ m___ g_____ l____ h_____   *I don't like eggs*

b. M__ e_____ l_____ m_____
I love apples

c. O_____ l____ h_____   *I hate burgers*

d. M___ g_____n m_____ l___ c_____
I like chocolates a lot

e. E__ c_____ e___ s_____   *coffee is tasty*

f. E__ p_____ e__ s_____   *fish is healthy*

g. E__ curry indio e__ p_____   *Indian curry is spicy*

5. Complete each sentence in a way which is logical and grammatically correct

a. Las _____ no son sanas

b. Los plátanos son _____

c. No me _____ la leche

d. Me _____ el pollo asado

e. _____ el pescado porque es sano

f. _____ la carne roja porque es malsana

g. _____ las verduras porque son sanas y deliciosas

Unit 11. Talking about food (Part 1): READING

¡Hola! Me llamo Roberto. ¿Qué prefiero comer? Me encanta el marisco, entonces me gustan mucho las gambas y los calamares porque son deliciosos. Me gusta mucho el pescado también porque es sabroso y rico en proteínas. Sobre todo el salmón. Me gusta bastante el pollo asado. Además, me gusta bastante la fruta, sobre todo los plátanos y las fresas. No me gustan mucho las verduras porque no son sabrosas.

¡Hola! Me llamo Alejandro. ¿Qué prefiero comer? Me encantan las verduras. Las como todos los días. Mis verduras preferidas son las espinacas, las zanahorias y las berenjenas porque son ricas en vitaminas y minerales. También me gusta la fruta porque es sana y deliciosa. Odio la carne y el pescado. Son ricos en proteínas pero no son sabrosos.

¡Hola! Me llamo Violeta. ¿Qué prefiero comer? Me encanta la carne, sobre todo la carne de cordero, porque es muy sabrosa. Me gusta mucho el pollo asado picante porque es sabroso y rico en proteínas. Me gustan bastante los huevos. Son sanos y ricos en vitaminas y proteínas. Me gusta bastante la fruta, sobre todo las cerezas. Son muy deliciosas y ricas en vitaminas. No me gustan nada las manzanas.

¡Hola! Me llamo Javier. ¿Qué prefiero comer? Prefiero la carne. Me encanta porque es sabrosa. Me gustan mucho las hamburguesas porque son sabrosas. También, me gusta mucho la fruta porque es dulce. No me gustan las verduras. Odio los tomates y las zanahorias. No aguanto los huevos. Son ricos en proteínas y vitaminas, pero son asquerosos. No me gustan las patatas fritas porque son muy malsanas.

¡Hola! Me llamo Fernando. ¿Qué prefiero comer? Me encanta la carne roja porque es muy sabrosa y rica en proteínas. No como mucho pescado porque no me gusta. Me gustan bastante los calamares fritos, pero no son sanos. Me gusta muchísimo la fruta, sobre todo los plátanos, porque son deliciosos, ricos en vitaminas y no son caros. No me gustan las manzanas y odio las naranjas. No como verduras.

1. Find the Spanish in Roberto's text

a. I love seafood

b. I like prawns

c. Are delicious

d. I like fish a lot

e. Salmon

f. I quite like

g. Moreover

h. Above all

i. They are not tasty

2. Fernando or Roberto? Write F or R next to each statement below

a. I love seafood - **Roberto**

b. I hate oranges

c. I like fruit a lot

d. I don't like vegetables

e. I prefer salmon

f. I quite like squid

g. I prefer bananas

h. I don't eat much fish

i. I love red meat

3. Complete the following sentences based on Alejandro's text

a. Alejandro loves_____

b. He eats them _____

c. His favourite vegetables are _____ _____ and _____

d. He also likes _____ because it is _____ and _____

e. He hates _____ and _____

4. Fill in the table below (in English) about Javier

Loves	Likes a lot	Doesn't like	Hates

Unit 11. Talking about food (Part 1): TRANSLATION

1. Faulty translation: spot and correct IN THE ENGLISH any translation mistakes you find below

a. Me encantan las gambas: *I hate prawns*

b. Odio el pollo : *I like meat*

c. Me gusta la miel: *I don't like honey*

d. Me encantan las naranjas: *I love apples*

e. Los huevos son asquerosos: *eggs are tasty*

f. Los plátanos son ricos en vitaminas: *bananas are rich in protein*

g. El pescado es muy sano: *fish is unhealthy*

h. Prefiero el agua mineral: *I prefer tap water*

i. Odio las verduras: *I love vegetables*

j. Me encanta el arroz: *I love rice pudding*

k. No me gusta la fruta: *I quite like fruit*

l. Los calamares fritos son sabrosos: *fried squid is salty*

2. Translate into English

a. Las gambas son sabrosas:

b. El pescado es delicioso:

c. El pollo es rico en proteínas:

d. Me encanta el arroz:

e. La carne roja es malsana:

f. Unos calamares fritos:

g. Los huevos son asquerosos:

h. Prefiero el agua con gas:

i. Me gustan bastante las gambas:

j. No me gustan las verduras:

k. Me gustan las zanahorias:

l. Este café es muy dulce:

m. Una manzana asquerosa:

n. Unas naranjas deliciosas:

3. Phrase-level translation En to Sp

a. Spicy chicken:

b. This coffee:

c. I quite like:

d. Very sweet:

e. A disgusting apple:

f. Some delicious oranges:

g. I don't like:

h. I love:

i. Tasty fish:

j. Mineral water:

k. Roast meat:

4. Sentence-level translation En to Sp

a. I like spicy chicken a lot

b. I like oranges because they are healthy

c. Meat is tasty but unhealthy

d. This coffee is very sweet

e. Eggs are disgusting

f. I love oranges. They are delicious and rich in vitamins

g. I love fish. It is tasty and rich in protein

h. Vegetables are disgusting

i. I prefer bananas

j. This tea is sweet

Unit 11. Talking about food (Part 1): WRITING

1. Split sentences

Me gusta el pollo	fruta
Odio las verduras porque	asado
Prefiero la	café es dulce
Este	son asquerosas
Me gusta bastante la	sabrosos pero malsanos
Los calamares fritos son	los plátanos
Me encantan	carne

2. Rewrite the sentences in the correct order

a. (Example) el Me asado pollo encanta
Me encanta el pollo asado

b. las verduras Odio

c. café Este dulce es

d. fritos Los malsanos son calamares

e. el mineral Prefiero agua

f. asquerosas son verduras Las

g. mucho las gustan naranjas Me son porque deliciosas

3. Spot and correct the grammar and spelling (there may be missing words)

a. Me gusta las naranjas

b. No gustan las verduras

c. Los huevos asquerosos

d. Me encanta este cafe

e. Prefero las zanahorias

f. Odio el carne

4. Anagrams

a. sArosoque

b. erudVasr

c. rneCa

d. escaPdo

e. anSo

f. ulDec

g. cheLe

5. Guided writing – write 4 short paragraphs describing the people below using the details in the box I

Person	Loves	Quite likes	Doesn't like	Hates
Natalia	Chorizo because spicy	Milk because healthy	Red meat	Eggs because disgusting
Iker	Chicken because healthy	Oranges because sweet	Fish	Meat because unhealthy
Julieta	Honey because sweet	Fish because tasty	Fruit	Vegetables because boring

6. Write a paragraph on Rafa in Spanish using the third person singular

Name: Rafa
Age: 18
Description: Tall, good-looking, sporty, nice
Occupation: Student
Food he loves: Chicken
Food he likes: Vegetables
Food he doesn't like: Red meat
Food he hates: Fish

Grammar Time 8: COMER/BEBER
Talking about food Part 1

Beber *to drink*			
Bebo	**agua**	*water*	
	café	*coffee*	
Bebes	**chocolate caliente**	*hot chocolate*	
Bebe	**leche**	*milk*	
	naranjada	*orangeade*	
Bebemos	**té**	*tea*	
Bebéis	**zumo de fruta**	*fruit juice*	
Beben	**zumo de manzana**	*apple juice*	**a menudo** *often*
Comer *to eat*			
	arroz	*rice*	**a veces** *sometimes*
	carne	*meat*	
	chocolate	*chocolate*	
	ensalada verde	*green salad*	**de vez en cuando**
Como	**fruta**	*fruit*	*from time to time*
	miel	*honey*	
Comes	**pan**	*bread*	**nunca** *never*
	pescado	*fish*	
Come	**pollo asado**	*roast chicken*	
	queso	*cheese*	**raramente** *rarely*
Comemos	**chocolates**	*chocolates*	
	gambas	*prawns*	**todos los días** *every day*
Coméis	**hamburguesas**	*burgers*	
	huevos	*eggs*	
	manzanas	*apples*	
Comen	**naranjas**	*oranges*	
	plátanos	*bananas*	
	tomates	*tomatoes*	
	verduras	*vegetables*	

THE LANGUAGE GYM

1. Match

Como	They eat
Comes	He/she eats
Come	We eat
Comemos	You guys eat
Coméis	You eat
Comen	I eat

2. Translate into English

a. Como pasta

b. Bebe zumo de pera

c. Nunca como carne

d. Come mucho pescado

e. Bebemos agua

f. Nunca comen pollo

g. Como arroz a menudo

h. ¿Comes pollo?

i. ¿Qué coméis?

j. Bebo zumo a menudo

3. Spot and correct the mistakes

a. Mi padre como pasta

b. Mi hermano y yo no comomos verduras

c. Mi madre nunca como chocolate

d. Mis hermanos bebe mucho zumo de fruta

e. (Yo) Nunca beben café

f. Mi hermana coma carne todos los días

g. ¿(Vosotros) Comen carne de caballo?

h. ¿Qué bebéis tú?

4. Complete

a. Mi padre _____ mucha fruta

b. (Yo) Nunca _____ zumo de kiwi

c. ¿(Tú) _____ pollo?

d. Mi madre y yo _____ mucha pasta

e. Mis padres _____ mucha agua

f. Mi hermana _____ mucho chocolate caliente

g. Mi novia nunca _____ vino

h. ¿(Vosotros) Qué _____ para el desayuno?

5. Translate into Spanish

a. I eat pasta

b. We drink orange juice

c. What do you eat?

d. What do you guys drink?

e. We eat a lot meat

f. They don't eat a lot of fish

g. She never eats vegetables

h. We drink lots of mineral water

6. Translate into Spanish

a. I never eat red meat. I don't like it because it is unhealthy.

b. I rarely eat sausages. I don't like them because they are oily.

c. I drink fruit juice often. I love it because it is delicious and healthy.

d. I eat paella every day. I love it because it is very tasty.

e. I rarely eat vegetables. They are tasty but I don't like them because they are disgusting.

f. I never drink tea or coffee because I don't like them.

UNIT 12
Talking about food - Part 2
Likes/ Dislikes / Reasons

Grammar Time: Agreement (food)

In this unit you will consolidate all that you learnt in the previous unit and learn how to say:
- What meals you eat every day and
- What you eat at each meal
- The full present indicative conjugation of 'tomar', 'desayunar', 'cenar'
- The full present indicative conjugation of 'almorzar'
- 'This' and 'these' in Spanish

You will revisit the following:
- The full present indicative conjugation of regular AR verbs
- Noun-to-adjective agreement

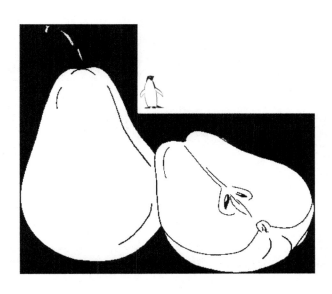

Unit 12 Part 2
Talking about food: Likes/ Dislikes / Reasons

Desayuno *At breakfast I eat* **Almuerzo** *At lunch I eat* **Meriendo** *At tea time I eat*	**el arroz** *rice* **el atún** *tuna fish* **el café** *coffee* **el chocolate** *chocolate* **el pescado** *fish* **el pollo asado** *roast chicken* **el queso** *cheese* **el salmón** *salmon* **el zumo de fruta** *fruit juice*	**porque es** *because it is*	**asqueroso** *disgusting* **amargo** *bitter* **delicioso** *delicious* **dulce** *sweet* **grasiento** *greasy* **ligero** *light* **picante** *spicy* **soso** *bland*
Ceno *At dinner I eat* **Bebo** *I drink*	**el agua** *water* **la carne** *meat* **la ensalada verde** *green salad* **la fruta** *fruit* **la leche** *milk* **la miel** *honey* **la paella** *paella*		**jugosa** *juicy* **malsana** *unhealthy* **refrescante** *refreshing* **rica en vitaminas** *rich in vitamins* **sabrosa** *tasty* **sana** *healthy*
Likes/dislikes **Me encantan** *I love* **Me gustan mucho** *I like a lot* **Me gustan** *I like*	**los bocadillos de queso** *cheese sandwiches* **los calamares** *squid* **los melocotones** *peaches* **los plátanos** *bananas* **los tomates** *tomatoes*	**porque son** *because they are*	**asquerosos** *disgusting* **amargos** *bitter* **deliciosos** *delicious* **ricos en vitaminas** *rich in vitamins*
Me gustan un poco *I like a bit* **No me gustan** *I don't like* **Odio** *I hate*	**las gambas** *prawns* **las hamburguesas** *burgers* **las manzanas** *apples* **las naranjas** *oranges* **las salchichas** *sausages* **las verduras** *vegetables*		**dulces** *sweet* **grasientas** *greasy* **refrescantes** *refreshing* **sabrosas** *tasty* **saladas** *salty* **sanas** *healthy*

Author's note: *Don't forget,* adjectives ending in 'e' do not change from masculine to feminine.

 **THE LANGUAGE GYM**

Unit 12. Talking about food – Likes/Dislikes (Part 2): VOCABULARY

1. Match

El agua	sandwich
El pescado	water
El arroz	roast chicken
El bocadillo	fish
El pollo asado	cheese
La carne	honey
Los calamares	prawns
Las gambas	strawberries
La miel	sausages
El queso	rice
Las salchichas	fruit
Las fresas	squid
Las verduras	vegetables
La fruta	meat

2. Complete with the missing words

a. Me gustan los _____   *I like seafood*

b. Me encanta la _____   *I love salad*

c. Me gustan mucho las _____   *I like vegetables*

d. Me gustan las _____   *I like apples*

e. Este _____ es delicioso   *This chicken is delicious*

f. Esta _____ es muy jugosa   *This meat is very juicy*

g. Me gustan mucho los _____   *I like bananas a lot*

h. Me encanta la _____   *I love honey*

i. No me gusta el _____   *I don't like fish*

3. Complete with the missing letters

a. El a_ _ _ _ water

b. La _ _ _ _ ne meat

c. La fr_ _ _ _ fruit

d. El l _ _ _ n lemon

e. La manza_ _ apple

f. La pat_ _ _ potato

g. Los mar_ _ _ _ _ _ seafood

h. La fr_ _ _ strawberry

i. Jug_ _ _ juicy

j. El pesc_ _ _ _ fish

k. Cas_ _ _ homemade

l. El ar_ _ _ _ rice

m. El hel_ _ _ _ ice cream

n. El melo_ _ _ _ _ _ peach

o. La cer_ _ _ _ cherry

p. Bu_ _ _ _ good

q. El p_ _ bread

r. Pi_ _ _ _ _ _ spicy

4. Match

Fuerte	Good
Frito	Delicious
Jugoso	Juicy
Sabroso	Healthy
Saludable	Strong
Bueno	Disgusting
Delicioso	Fried
Grasiento	Sweet
Asqueroso	Greasy
Dulce	Tasty
Amargo	Bitter

5. Sort the items below into the appropriate category

a. delicioso	e. bueno	i. manzana	m. amargo	q. salmón	u. leche
b. saludable	f. gambas	j. fresa	n. carne	r. pollo	v. melocotones
c. rico	g. grasiento	k. asqueroso	o. atún	s. dulce	w. zanahorias
d. jugoso	h. malsano	l. plátanos	p. sano	t. espinacas	x. queso

Fruta	Verdura	Adjetivos	Pescado y carne	Productos lácteos

THE LANGUAGE GYM

Unit 12. Talking about food – Likes/Dislikes (Part 2): READING

Me llamo Roberto. ¿Qué como? Por lo general no desayuno mucho. Solo una manzana o un plátano y un poco de café. No me gusta el café dulce.

A mediodía, por lo general, almuerzo una hamburguesa con patatas fritas y bebo agua o zumo de fruta. Las hamburguesas no son sanas, pero me chiflan. Me encanta el zumo de fresa.

Después del colegio meriendo dos tostadas con mermelada y mantequilla y bebo una taza de té. Para la cena como bastante. Suelo comer arroz, marisco o pollo con verduras y de postre uno o dos pasteles. Me gustaría comer queso, porque es delicioso, pero mi madre dice que no es sano. Ella odia el queso.

Me llamo Fernando. ¿Qué como? Por lo general no desayuno mucho. Solo un huevo y una taza de té. El té me gusta dulce, con mucho azúcar. A veces bebo zumo de piña.

A mediodía almuerzo pollo asado con verduras y bebo agua mineral. Como muchas verduras porque son muy sanas y deliciosas. Me gustaría comer gambas porque me encantan.

Después del colegio meriendo dos tostadas con miel y bebo una taza de té. Me encanta la miel porque es muy dulce, deliciosa y es rica en vitaminas.

Para la cena como bastante. Suelo comer arroz, mariscos o pescado con verduras y de postre uno o dos pasteles. A veces como pollo porque es rico en proteínas, pero no me gusta mucho porque no es muy sabroso.

1. Find the Spanish for the words below in Fernando's text.

a. Egg : h_____

b. Tea: t_____

c. Sweet: d_____

d. Sugar: a_____

e. Noon: m_____

f. Chicken: p_____

g. Roast: a_____

h. After: d_____

i. Cup: t_____

j. Honey: m_____

k. Vegetables: v_____

l. Healthy: s_____

m. Delicious: d_____

n. Dinner: c_____

o. Tasty: s_____

p. Pastries: p_____

2. Complete the following sentences based on Fernando's text

a. In general, at breakfast I only eat an _____ and a cup of _____

b. I like tea _____ with a lot of _____

c. At _____, for lunch I eat _____ _____ with _____ and drink _____ _____

d. I eat a lot of vegetables because they are _____ and delicious

e. As a snack I have two _____ with _____ and drink a _____ of tea

f. At dinner I usually eat _____, seafood or _____ with _____ and for dessert, one or two _____.

g. Sometimes I eat _____

3. Find the Spanish for the following in Roberto/Fernando's text

a. I don't have much for breakfast

b. At noon I eat

c. Roast chicken

d. For dessert

e. One or two pastries

f. I would like to eat

g. A cup of tea

h. After school

i. Rice, seafood or fish

j. Toasts with jam

k. Burgers are not healthy

l. Very sweet

m. An apple or a banana

4. Who says this, Roberto or Fernando? Or both?

a. I would love to eat cheese – *Roberto*

b. I love honey

c. I love strawberry juice

d. I don't eat much for breakfast

e. I would like to eat prawns

f. I have toasts with jam and butter

g. I am crazy about burgers

h. Burgers are not healthy

i. At dinner I eat quite a bit

j. I drink mineral water

k. His mother hates cheese

l. Sometimes I drink pineapple juice

Me llamo Eugenio. ¿Qué como? Por lo general por la mañana como mucho; un plátano, dos o tres huevos, tostadas con jamón, un zumo de fruta y una taza de café. El café me gusta dulce.

A mediodía, por lo general, almuerzo solo arroz con pollo o verduras y bebo agua mineral o zumo de naranja. Me encanta el pollo porque es sano y es rico en proteínas. A veces como espárragos. Me encantan porque son amargos y ricos en vitaminas.

Después del colegio meriendo dos tostadas con mermelada y mantequilla y bebo una taza de té.

Para la cena como mucho. Suelo comer pasta, carne con verduras y de postre helado o pasteles. Me gustaría comer chocolate, porque es delicioso, pero mi madre dice que no es sano.

5. Answer the following questions on Eugenio's text

a. How much does he eat at breakfast?

b. What does he eat? 4 things

c. How does he like coffee?

d. What juice does he drink at lunch?

e. What does he have with rice?

f. Why does he like asparagus?

g. What does he put on toasts in the afternoon?

h. Why doesn't his mother allow him to eat chocolate?

---

6. Find in Eugenio's text the following:

a. a word for dessert, starting with P:

b. a vegetable starting with E:

c. a drink starting with Z:

d. a type of cold meat starting with J:

e. a fruit starting with P:

f. a dairy product starting with M:

g. an adjective starting with S:

h. a container starting with T:

i. a verb starting with C:

j. a fruit starting with N:

k. an adjective starting with R:

l. a meal starting with M:

THE LANGUAGE GYM

Unit 12. Talking about food – Likes/Dislikes (Part 2): WRITING

1. Split sentences

Siempre como pollo	con leche
Desayuno cereales	mantequilla
Tomo una tostada con	asado
Me gusta la ensalada	fruta favorita
La carne roja es	deliciosa pero malsana
El curry es	o café
El plátano es mi	verde
Bebo té	muy picante

2. Complete with the correct option

a. Me encanta el _____, sobre todo los calamares.

b. Por lo general, _____ arroz con pollo

c. Normalmente _____cereales, en la cocina

d. Siempre almuerzo _____ asado con mi hermano

e. Ceno pescado y una ensalada_____.

f. Normalmente, meriendo un bocadillo de _____.

g. Me gusta mucho la _____ porque es muy dulce

h. El café es _____, pero me encanta.

i. No me _____ la leche, ¡qué asco!

j. La fruta es dulce y_____.

verde	pollo	almuerzo	queso	amargo
miel	marisco	desayuno	gusta	ligera

3. Spot and correct the grammar and spelling mistakes note: in several cases a word is missing

a. Por lo general, almwerzo una hamburguesa con patata fritas

b. Bebo agua o zumo fruta.

c. La carne roja no es sanas, pero me gustan.

d. Me encantan el zumo de naranja.

e. Después del colegio meriendo dos tostada miel

f. Bebo un taza de té con leche.

g. Me encanto la miel porque es delicioso y es rica en vitamina.

h. Para la cena yo comes arroz or pescado con verduras.

i. Me encantan las verduras porque son sanos

j. Mi pescado favorito es el salmón. ¡Es deliciosa!

4. Complete the words

a. Al_____ *lunch*

b. C_____ *dinner*

c. D_____ *breakfast*

d. P_____ *spicy*

e. A_____ *bitter*

f. D_____ *sweet*

g. S_____ *healthy*

6. Sentence level translation EN - SP

a. I love fruit juice because it is sweet and refreshing.

b. I don't like salmon because it is disgusting.

c. At tea time I eat a cheese sandwich.

d. I always drink milk with honey. I like it because it's sweet.

e. I like fish, but chicken is not very tasty.

5. Guided writing – write 3 short paragraphs in the first person I using the details below

Person	Lunch	Location	With	After *(y luego)*
Elías	Chicken and rice	The kitchen	Brother	Go to the beach
Santino	Burger	The dining room	Sister	Read a book
Julieta	Salad	The garden	Mother	Listen to music

Grammar Time 9: AR Verbs (Part 2)
DESAYUNAR, CENAR, TOMAR and ALMORZAR

DESAYUNAR *to eat for breakfast*	CENAR *to eat for dinner*	agua un bistec *a steak*
Desayun<u>o</u> *I have... for breakfast*	Ceno *I eat...for dinner*	un café carne cereales con leche
Desayun<u>as</u> *you...*	Cenas	fruta
Desayun<u>a</u> *she/he...*	Cena	gambas
Desayun<u>amos</u> *we...*	Cenamos	huevos *eggs*
Desayun<u>áis</u> *you guys...*	Cenáis	leche marisco
Desayun<u>an</u> *they...*	Cenan	mermelada
TOMAR *to "have"*	ALMORZAR * *to eat for lunch*	miel *honey* pan
Tomo *I "have"*	Almuerzo *I eat...for lunch*	pescado pollo
Tomas	Almuerzas	queso
Toma	Almuerza	un plátano
Tomamos	<u>Almorzamos</u>	salchichas
Tomáis	<u>Almorzáis</u>	una tostada verduras
Toman	Almuerzan	zumo de fruta

Author's note: Tomar is a really handy verb. In the context of food and drink it means the same as to have: like the English "I have a coffee" or "I have some bread for lunch"

DRILLS

1. Complete with the missing letters

a. (yo) Desayun__ cereales con leche

b. Mi madre tom__ un café

c. Mis padres tom__ __ un té

d. Mi padre almuerz__ arroz con pollo

e. Mis hermanas no cen__ __ mucho

f. (yo) Almuerz__ fruta o ensalada

g. ¿Qué almuerz__ __ tú?

h. ¿Qué cena__ ellos?

i. Mis padres no desayun__ __

j. A mediodía mi amigo Paco cen__ carne

k. Mi hermano y yo cen__ __ __ __ muy poco

l. Mi hermano mayor desayun__ tres huevos

THE LANGUAGE GYM

2. Complete with the missing forms of 'Desayunar'

a. (yo) No _____ mucho. Solo tomo un café

b. Mi madre solo _____ una fruta

c. Mis padres solo _____ una tostada con mermelada

d. Mi hermana _____ cereales con leche

e. Mi hermano y yo _____ dos tostadas con mantequilla

f. ¿Qué _____ tú?

g. Y vosotros, ¿qué _____?

3. Spot and correct the errors with the verbs 'Tomar', 'Almorzar' and 'Cenar'

a. (yo) No toma café

b. Mi madre cenas un bistec y verduras

c. Mi hermano y yo no almuerzan

d. Mi padre nunca tomo alcohol

e. Mi amigo Paco nunca toman el desayuno

f. Mi novia y yo tomáis un café con leche en la cantina del colegio

g. Mi novia nunca cenan carne roja

4. Translate into English

a. Mi madre nunca almuerza

b. Mi hermana nunca almuerza un bistec

c. A veces tomo café con leche

d. Por lo general tomamos huevos para el desayuno

e. ¿Qué almuerzas normalmente?

f. Solo desayuno una o dos tostadas y una taza de café

g. Para el desayuno mis hermanos toman cereales con leche

6. Translate into Spanish

a. For breakfast I have two eggs and one sausage. Also, I have a coffee with milk.

b. My friend Paco doesn't have much for lunch. Only chicken with rice.

c. For dinner we eat a lot. We have a steak or fish with potatoes.

d. At noon I have a cup of coffee in the canteen with my girlfriend.

e. My girlfriend never has red meat. She only eats fish or chicken.

f. My parents eat a lot for lunch. However, my brother and I eat only a salad.

g. My sisters don't eat much for dinner. Generally, they have soup or vegetables.

5. Translate into Spanish

a. For dinner I eat: C_____

b. For lunch we eat: A_____

c. For breakfast she has: D_____

d. They have: T_____

e. She has: T_____

f. For dinner we eat: C_____

g. For lunch you have: A_____

h. For breakfast they have: D_____

Grammar Time 10: AGREEMENTS (Part 2) (Food)

El *The* **Este** *This*	cerdo *(pork)* chocolate *marisco *(seafood)* pescado pan pollo queso zumo de fruta	**es** *is*	asqueroso bueno delicioso **dulce** grasiento malsano **picante** sabroso salado sano
La *The* **Esta** *This*	carne ensalada fruta mermelada miel		asquerosa buena deliciosa **dulce** grasienta malsana **picante** sabrosa salada sana
Los *The* **Estos** *These*	bombones *(chocolates)* dulces *(sweets)* mariscos *(seafood)* pasteles plátanos refrescos *(fizzy drinks)*	**son** *are*	asquerosos buenos deliciosos **dulces** grasientos malsanos **picantes** sabrosos salados sanos
Las *The* **Estas** *These*	fresas *(strawberries)* gambas manzanas salchichas verduras		asquerosas buenas deliciosas **dulces** grasientas malsanas **picantes** sabrosas saladas sanas

Author's note: *Some regions favour keeping "marisco" (seafood) always in the singular; other regions use it as a simple noun and also have the plural "mariscos". Both are officially correct.*

 **THE LANGUAGE GYM**

1. Choose the correct option as shown in the example

	A	B
El pescado es	**sano**	sana
Este pan es	delicioso	deliciosa
Esta carne es	duro	dura
La leche es	asquerosa	asqueroso
El cerdo es	grasiento	grasienta
Esta manzana es	asqueroso	asquerosa
Esta fresa es	dulce	dulcea
Los mariscos son	sanos	sanas

2. Write the opposite version of the adjectives below

Masculino	Femenino
	asquerosa
delicioso	
	grasienta
dulce	
picante	
	sana
dulces	
picantes	

3. Translate into English

a. Estas gambas son asquerosas

b. Estas fresas son deliciosas

c. Estos mariscos son muy sabrosos

d. Esta manzana es repugnante

e. Este pescado es muy bueno

f. Este pollo es demasiado picante

4. Tick the grammatically correct sentences and correct the incorrect ones

a. Estas gambas son muy sabrosos

b. Este cordero es muy bueno

c. Este pollo es muy salados

d. Esta manzana es muy deliciosa

e. Los mariscos son muy sanas

f. Estas salchichas son muy grasientas

5. Complete

a. El pescado es asqueros___

b. Las manzanas son san____

c. La carne roja es malsan____

d. Los pasteles son demasiado dulc____

e. Los mariscos son muy san____

f. Estas fresas son delicios____

g. Estos plátanos son muy delicios____

h. Estas gambas son asqueros____

6. Translate into Spanish

a. This fish is disgusting

b. These prawns are delicious

c. This coffee is too sweet

d. These sausages are very fatty

e. These vegetables are very tasty

f. Oranges are very healthy

g. This paella is very good

Question Skills 2: Jobs/School bag/Food

1. Translate into English

a. ¿Dónde comes a mediodía?

b. ¿Qué trabajo hace tu madre?

c. ¿Qué hay en tu mochila?

d. ¿Cuál es tu comida preferida?

e. ¿Cuál es tu bebida preferida?

f. ¿Con qué frecuencia comes carne?

g. ¿Te gusta el zumo de fruta?

h. ¿Por qué no comes verduras?

i. ¿Comes dulces a menudo?

j. ¿Qué trabajo te gustaría hacer?

k. ¿Cómo es tu hermana?

l. ¿Con quién desayunas por lo general?

2. Match the answers below to the questions in activity 1

1. El zumo de manzana   __e__

2. Es inteligente y muy graciosa   _____

3. Me gustaría ser jardinero   _____

4. Sí. Me encanta. Es delicioso   _____

5. Porque no me gustan   _____

6. La paella   _____

7. Sí. Todos los días   _____

8. La como dos veces por semana   _____

9. Hay dos cuadernos y una agenda   _____

10. Mi madre es policía   _____

11. En la cantina del colegio   _____

12. Solo   _____

3. Provide the questions to the following answers

a. No como carne

b. Siempre como verduras porque son sanas

c. Trabajo como bombero

d. Me encanta la fruta porque es deliciosa y sana

e. Juego al fútbol en el colegio

f. Como marisco a menudo

g. Como cinco porciones de fruta al día

h. Soy de Colombia

i. No tengo mascotas

j. Mi bebida preferida es el zumo de manzana

k. Mi padre trabaja como abogado

l. En mi estuche solo hay dos lápices

4. Complete

a. ¿Q_____ h_____ e__ t__ mochila?

b. ¿Q____ t_____ haces?

c. ¿C_____ q__ f_____ comes marisco?

d. ¿C_____ e___ t__ carne preferida?

e. ¿C_____ e__ t__ bebida p_____?

f. ¿P__ q_____ n__ t__ g_____ la carne?

g. ¿D__ d_____ eres?

h. ¿C____ q_____ desayunas normalmente?

UNIT 13
Talking about clothes and accessories I wear, how frequently and when

Grammar Time 11: -AR Verbs (Part 2) Llevar + Agreements

Revision Quickie 3: Jobs, food, clothes and numbers 20-100

In this unit you will learn how to:

- Say what clothes you wear in various circumstances and places
- Describe various types of weather
- Give a wide range of words for clothing items and accessories
- Use a range of words for places in town
- Make the full present indicative conjugation of 'llevar' (to wear)

You will revisit:
- Time markers
- Frequency markers
- Colours
- Self-introduction phrases
- Present indicative of 'Tener'
- Noun-to-adjective agreement

UNIT 13
Talking about clothes

Cuando hace calor *When it is hot* **Cuando hace frío** *When it is cold* **Cuando salgo con mi novio/novia** *When I go out with my boyfriend/girlfriend* **Cuando salgo con mis padres** *When I go out with my parents* **Cuando salgo con mis amigos** *When I go out with my friends* **Cuando juego al fútbol** *When I play football* **En casa** *At home* **En la discoteca** *At the nightclub* **En el colegio** *at school* **En el gimnasio** *at the gym* **En la playa** *at the beach* **Nunca** *never* **Por lo general** *usually* **Siempre** *always*	**llevo** *I wear* **lleva** *he/she wears*	**una bufanda** *a scarf* **una chaqueta** *a jacket* **una camisa** *a shirt* **una camiseta** *a t-shirt* **una camiseta sin mangas** *tank top / vest* **una chaqueta deportiva** *a sports jacket* **una corbata** *a tie* **una falda** *a skirt* **una gorra** *a baseball cap*	**azul** *blue* **blanca** *white* **gris** *grey* **amarilla** *yellow* **marrón** *brown* **naranja** *orange* **negra** *black* **roja** *red* **verde** *green*
		un abrigo *a coat* **un bañador** *a swimsuit* **un chaleco** *a waistcoat* **un chándal** *a tracksuit* **un cinturón** *a belt* **un collar** *a necklace* **un jersey** *jumper* **un reloj** *a watch* **un sombrero** *a hat* **un top** *a top* **un traje** *a suit* **un uniforme** *a uniform* **un vestido** *a dress*	**azul** *blue* **blanco** *white* **gris** *grey* **amarillo** *yellow* **marrón** *brown* **naranja** *orange* **negro** *black* **rojo** *red* **verde** *green*
		botas *boots* **calcetines** *socks* **pantalones** *trousers* **pantalones cortos** *shorts* **pantuflas** *slippers* **pendientes** *earrings* **sandalias** *sandals* **vaqueros** *jeans* **zapatos** *shoes* **zapatos de tacón** *high heel shoes* **zapatillas de deporte** *sports shoes*	**azules** *blue* **blancos/as** *white* **grises** *grey* **amarillos/as** *yellow* **marrones** *brown* **naranja** *orange* **negros/as** *black* **rojos/as** *red* **verdes** *green*

Unit 13. Talking about clothes: VOCABULARY BUILDING

1. Match up

Unos pendientes	A baseball cap
Una camiseta	Shoes
Un vestido	Trousers
Unos zapatos	A suit
Un pantalón	A T-shirt
Un traje	Earrings
Una gorra	A dress

2. Translate into English

a. Llevo una camiseta negra

b. Llevo un traje gris

c. No llevo zapatillas de deporte

d. Llevo una gorra azul

e. No llevo un reloj

f. Nunca llevo pendientes

g. Llevo un chándal

h. Nunca llevo trajes

i. Siempre llevo sandalias

j. Nunca llevo sombreros

k. Mi hermano siempre lleva vaqueros

3. Complete with the missing word

a. En casa _____ una _____
At home I wear a T-shirt

b. En el colegio llevo un _____ _____
At school I wear a black uniform

c. En el gimnasio _____ un chándal _____
At the gym I wear a pink tracksuit

d. En la _____ llevo un _____
At the beach I wear a swimsuit

e. ___ ___ discoteca llevo un _____ negro
In the club I wear a black dress

f. Raramente _____ zapatillas ___ _____
I rarely wear sports shoes

g. Nunca _____ trajes *I never wear suits*

4. Anagrams clothes and accessories

a. una rrago

b. un lojre

c. un jetra

d. unos dntieespen

e. unos topasza

f. una setacami

g. unos roquesva

h. un lecocha

i. unas puntaflas

j. un stidove

k. un brerosom

l. un llarco

5. Associations – match each body part below with the words in the box

a. La cabeza *(head)* – e.g. **gorra**

b. Los pies *(feet)* –

c. Las piernas *(legs)* -

d. El cuello *(neck)* –

e. El torso *(upper body)* –

f. Las orejas *(ears)* –

g. La muñeca *(wrist)* –

bufanda	corbata	zapatos	botas
chaqueta	camisa	calcetines	**gorra**
pendientes	pantalones	falda	sombrero
chaleco	reloj	collar	camiseta

6. Complete

a. Llevo bo_____   *I wear boots*

b. En c_____   *At home*

c. Tengo un r_____   *I have a watch*

d. Llevo una c_____ roja   *I wear a red tie*

e. Llevo un t_____ azul   *I wear a blue suit*

f. Mi hermano lleva un ch_____
My brother wears a waistcoat

g. Ella siempre lleva vestidos n_____s
She always wears black dresses

Unit 13. Talking about clothes: READING

Me llamo Conchita. Soy de España. Tengo quince años. Soy muy deportista, entonces tengo mucha ropa de colores y estilos diferentes. Prefiero la ropa de buena calidad pero no muy cara. Por lo general, en casa llevo un chándal. Tengo cuatro o cinco chándales diferentes. Cuando salgo con mi novio llevo pendientes, un collar, un vestido rojo o negro y zapatos de tacón.

Me llamo Renaud. Soy de Francia. Tengo trece años. Me encanta comprar ropa, sobre todo zapatos. Tengo muchos zapatos de marca. Me encanta la ropa italiana. Cuando hace frío, por lo general llevo un abrigo y pantalones negros o morados. A veces llevo una chaqueta deportiva. Cuando hace calor llevo camisas sin mangas, vaqueros y sandalias o zapatillas de deporte. En mi casa tengo un caballo que se llama Jacques Chirac.

Me llamo Gerda. Soy de Alemania. Tengo doce años. Siempre compro la ropa de Zara. Me gusta la ropa bonita pero no demasiado cara. La ropa de marca no me gusta. Siempre llevo ropa deportiva como chándales, camisetas sin mangas y zapatillas de deportes. Cuando hace frío llevo una chaqueta deportiva y chándal. Cuando hace calor llevo una camiseta y pantalones cortos.

Me llamo Miguel. Soy de Argentina. Tengo catorce años. Cuando voy al colegio llevo una camisa, pantalones y zapatos. En casa por lo general llevo una camiseta y vaqueros. Tengo muchas camisetas y vaqueros en casa. Cuando voy al gimnasio llevo una camiseta sin mangas, pantalones cortos y zapatillas de deporte. Cuando voy al centro comercial con mis amigos llevo una chaqueta, una camisa, unos pantalones negros o grises, y zapatos negros.

1. Find the Spanish in Conchita's text

a. I am from

b. Sporty

c. Many clothes

d. Good quality clothes

e. A tracksuit

f. When I go out

g. With my boyfriend

h. Earrings

i. A red or black dress

j. High heel shoes

2. Find the Spanish for the following in Miguel's text

a. When I go

b. I wear a shirt

c. T-shirt and jeans

d. At home

e. Tank top

f. With my friends

g. A jacket

h. Black trousers

i. Sports shoes

j. In general

3. Complete the following statements about Renaud

a. He is _____ years old

b. He loves buying _____

c. He has many branded _____

d. When it's cold he wears a _____ __ _____ or _____ _____

e. Sometimes he wears a_____ _____

4. Answer the questions about Gerda (in Spanish)

a. ¿Cómo se llama?

b. ¿De dónde es?

c. ¿Cuántos años tiene?

d. ¿Qué le gusta?

e. ¿Dónde compra su ropa?

f. ¿Qué ropa lleva cuando hace frío?

g. ¿Qué ropa lleva cuando hace calor?

5. Find Someone Who...

a. ...loves branded clothes

b. ...is from Germany

c. ...wears tank tops in the gym

d. ...wears earrings when she goes out with her boyfriend

e. ...has four or five different tracksuits

f. ...has a lot of T-shirts and jeans at home

g. ...is very sporty

h. ...wears grey or black trousers at the shopping mall

 THE LANGUAGE GYM

Unit 13. Talking about clothes: WRITING

1. Split sentences

En	camiseta y pantalones cortos
Cuando hace	casa llevo un chándal
En el gimnasio llevo una	llevo zapatos de tacón
Cuando hace calor llevo	frío llevo una bufanda
Nunca llevo vaqueros	una camiseta sin mangas
Cuando voy a la discoteca	Levi's
Llevo pantalones	negra
Llevo una camisa	negros

2. Complete with the correct option

a. _____ salgo con mi _____ llevo ropa bonita pero cómoda.

b. En el colegio _____ un uniforme azul

c. En el gimnasio llevo _____ de deporte

d. En la playa llevo un _____

e. Cuando _____ calor llevo una _____ sin mangas

f. En casa llevo ____ chándal

g. Cuando hace mucho frío llevo un _____

h. _____ llevo botas

abrigo	novio	un	llevo	cuando
zapatillas	nunca	hace	bañador	camiseta

3. Spot and correct the grammar and spelling mistakes note: in several cases a word is missing

a. Cuando salgo mis padres llevo un vestido elegante

b. En casa llevo una chándal

c. Tengo mucho zapatos

d. Mi hermano siempre llevo vaqueros

e. En el colegio un uniforme

f. Me da igual las ropas de marca

g. Cuando voy al centro commercial, por lo general llevo un chaqueta deportiva

h. Siempre llevo zapatillas deporte

4. Complete the words

a. F_____ skirt

b. T_____ suit

c. P_____ earrings

d. P_____ trousers

e. Z_____ shoes

f. B_____ scarf

g. C_____ tracksuit

6. Describe this person in Spanish using the 3rd person

Name: Juan

Lives in: London

Age : 20

Pet: A black spider

Hair: Blond

Eyes: Green

Always wears: A suit

Never wears: Jeans

At the gym wears: An Adidas tracksuit

5. Guided writing – write 3 short paragraphs in the first person I using the details below

Person	Lives	Always wears	Never wears	Hates
Amparo	Madrid	Black dresses	Trousers	Earrings
Jorge	Pamplona	White T-shirts	Coats	Watches
Julio	Valencia	Jeans	Shorts	Scarves

Grammar Time 11: AR Verbs (Part 3)
LLEVAR + TENER + AGREEMENTS

LLEVAR *to wear*

llevo *I wear*

llevas *you wear*

lleva *s/he wears*

llevamos *we wear*

lleváis *you guys wear*

llevan *they wear*

TENER *to have*

tengo *I have*

tienes *you have*

tiene *s/he has*

tenemos *we have*

tenéis *you guys have*

tienen *they have*

una bufanda *a scarf*	
una blusa *a blouse*	
una chaqueta *a jacket*	
una camisa *a shirt*	
una camiseta *a t-shirt*	
una corbata *a tie*	
una falda *a skirt*	
una gorra *a baseball cap*	

amarilla *yellow*

azul *blue*

blanca *white*

gris *grey*

marrón *brown*

naranja *orange*

negra *black*

roja *red*

verde *green*

un abrigo *a coat*

un bañador *a swimsuit*

un chaleco *a waistcoat*

un chándal *a tracksuit*

un cinturón *a belt*

un collar *a necklace*

un jersey *jumper*

un reloj *a watch*

un sombrero *a hat*

un top *a top*

un traje *a suit*

un uniforme *a uniform*

un vestido *a dress*

amarillo

azul

blanco

gris

marrón

naranja

negro

rojo

verde

DRILLS

1. Complete with the missing verb endings

a. (yo) Nunca llev__ faldas

b. ¿Qué ropa llev___ tú?

c. Mi hermano tien____ muchas camisetas

d. Mis padres llev____ ropa de marca

e. Mi profe de arte llev__ ropa muy fea

f. Mi amigo Paco tien__ mucha ropa guay

g. En el instituto llev_____ uniformes

h. (yo) ten____ muchos vaqueros

i. ¿Qué ropa llev_____? (vosotros)

j. Mi madre y yo ten_____ mucha ropa

k. (ella) Nunca llev__ vestidos elegantes

l. Cuando hace frío, (yo) llev__ una bufanda

2. Complete with the missing verbs

a. Mi madre _____ mucha ropa de marca — *My mother has a lot of branded clothes*

b. Mis hermanos también _____ camisetas — *My brothers also wear T-shirts*

c. Mi hermana por lo general _____ vaqueros — *My sister usually wears jeans*

d. Mis profesores siempre _____ trajes — *My teachers always wear suits*

e. Mi novia _____ muchos pendientes — *My girlfriend has many earrings*

f. Nosotros _____ una camiseta negra — *We have a black T-shirt*

g. Mis padres _____ mucha ropa deportiva — *My parents wear a lot of sporty clothes*

h. Mis primos no _____ mucha ropa — *My cousins don't have many clothes*

---

3. Complete with the correct form of 'llevar'

a. (yo) llev__ una camiseta

b. Mi madre llev__ un vestido elegante

c. Mis padres no llev___ ropa de marca

d. Mis hermanos llev__ vaqueros y camisetas

e. Mi hermano y yo llev____ ropa deportiva

f. Mi hermana nunca llev___ faldas

g. ¿Qué ropa llev___ tú?

h. (nosotros) Nunca llev_____ gorras

i. En el gimnasio (yo) llev____ un chándal

---

4. Complete with the correct form of 'tener'

a. (yo) No ten____ muchas camisetas

b. Nosotros no ten_____ ropa de marca

c. Mi hermano tien____ muchas camisetas negras

d. Mi amigo Paco no ti_____ mucha ropa (porque es un caballo)

e. Mis hermanos tie_____ muchas corbatas

f. Mi madre tie____ muchos vestidos elegantes.

---

5. Translate into English

a. Nunca llevo camisetas

b. Siempre lleva vaqueros

c. No tenemos vestidos elegantes

d. Tiene muchos zapatos

e. Tienen muchos zapatos de marca

f. Siempre llevan zapatillas de deporte

g. ¿Qué ropa llevas en el instituto?

h. En el gimnasio lleva un chándal

i. ¿Tenéis gorras de Adidas?

---

6. Translate into Spanish

a. Do you have baseball caps?

b. We have many shoes

c. I don't have an elegant dress

d. My father has many suits and ties

e. My mother never wears jeans

f. I never wear trainers

g. What clothes do you wear generally?

h. They never wear uniforms

i. At the gym I wear a tracksuit

j. Do you wear sports clothes often?

Revision Quickie 3: Jobs, food, clothes and numbers 20-100

1. Complete (numbers)

a. 100 ci

b. 90 no

c. 30 tr

d. 50 ci

e. 80 oc

f. 60 se

g. 40 cu

2. Translate into English (food and clothes)

a. el traje

b. la bebida

c. el pollo

d. la falda

e. el cerdo

f. el agua

g. la carne

h. los mariscos

i. el pescado

j. la bufanda

k. los zapatos

l. las verduras

m. el zumo

n. la cena

3. Write in a word for each letter in the categories below as shown in the example (there is no obvious word for the greyed out boxes!)

LETRA	Ropa	Comida y Bebidas	Numeros	Trabajos
S	sombrero	salchichas	sesenta	soldado
T				
V				
M				
A				

4. Match

Llevo	My name is
Tengo	I drink
Soy	For breakfast i have
Meriendo	I live
Como	I work
Bebo	I have
Desayuno	For dinner i have
Trabajo	There is
Ceno	I am
Vivo	For snack i have
Hay	I wear
Me llamo	I eat

5. Translate into English

a. Nunca llevo faldas

b. Siempre meriendo tostadas con miel

c. Trabajo como dependiente

d. Bebo café a menudo

e. No tomo refrescos

f. Siempre desayuno huevos

g. Mi madre es mujer de negocios

h. No tengo mucha ropa de marca

i. No ceno mucho. Solo una ensalada

UNIT 14
Saying what I and others do in our free time

Grammar Time: Hacer, Jugar, Ir

In this unit you will learn how to say:

- What activities you do using the verbs 'jugar' (play), 'hacer' (do) and 'ir' (go)
- Other free time activities

You will revisit:
- Time and frequency markers
- Weather
- Expressing likes/dislikes
- Adjectives
- Pets

UNIT 14
Saying what I (and others) do
in our free time

juego *I play*	**al ajedrez** *chess* **al baloncesto** *basketball* **a las cartas** *cards* **al fútbol** *football* **al tenis** tennis **con mis amigos** *with my friends*	**a menudo** *often* **a veces** *sometimes*
hago *I do*	**ciclismo** *cycling* **deporte** *sport* **equitación** *horse riding* **escalada** *rock climbing* **esquí** *skiing* **footing** *jogging* **natación** *swimming* **los deberes** *homework* **pesas** *weights* **senderismo** *hiking*	**casi nunca** *hardly ever* **cuando hace mal tiempo** *when the weather is bad* **cuando hace buen tiempo** *when the weather is good* **dos veces por semana** *twice a week*
voy *I go*	**a casa de mi amigo/a** *to my friend's house* **a la montaña** *to the mountain* **a la piscina** *to the pool* **a la playa** *to the beach* **al gimnasio** *to the gym* **al parque** *to the park* **al polideportivo** *to the sports centre* **de marcha** *clubbing* **de pesca** *fishing* **en bici** *on a bike ride*	**raramente** *rarely* **todos los días** *every day*

Unit 14. Free time: VOCABULARY BUILDING – Part 1 Weather

1. Match up

Juego al ajedrez	I go horse-riding
Hago footing	I play chess
Hago equitación	I play basketball
Juego a las cartas	I go hiking
Voy en bici	I go swimming
Hago natación	I go biking
Hago senderismo	I go jogging
Juego al baloncesto	I play cards

2. Complete with the missing word

a. Juego al _____ *I play chess*

b. _____ equitación *I go horse riding*

c. _____ a las cartas *I play cards*

d. Voy en _____ *I go cycling*

e. Juego al _____ *I play basketball*

f. Voy de _____ *I go fishing*

g. Hago _____ *I go hiking*

h. Hago _____ *I go rock climbing*

i. Hago _____ *I go jogging*

j. No hago los _____ *I don't do my homework*

juego	baloncesto	pesca	escalada	hago
deberes	bici	ajedrez	senderismo	footing

3. Translate into English

a. Voy en bici todos los días

b. Hago senderismo a menudo

c. Hago escalada dos veces por semana

d. Casi nunca hago equitación

e. Cuando hace mal tiempo juego a las cartas o al ajedrez

f. Juego al baloncesto a menudo

g. Voy de marcha raramente

h. Voy a casa de mi amigo a menudo

i. Voy a la playa todos los días

j. Voy de pesca una vez por semana

k. Juego al golf cuando hace buen tiempo

4. Broken words

a. Hago eq_____ *I go horse-riding*

b. Hago na_____ *I go swimming*

c. Voy de pe_____ *I go fishing*

d. Voy en bi_____ *I go biking*

e. Juego al aj_____ *I play chess*

f. Voy de ma_____ *I go clubbing*

g. Juego a las ca_____ *I play cards*

h. Hago esc_____ *I do rock climbing*

5. 'Voy', 'Juego' or 'Hago'?

a. _____ al baloncesto

b. _____ en bici

c. _____ al ajedrez

d. _____ a las cartas

e. _____ natación

f. _____ de marcha

g. _____ al tenis

h. _____ pesas

i. _____ escalada

6. Bad translation – spot any translation errors and fix them

a. Nunca voy de marcha : *I often go clubbing*

b. Juego a las cartas a menudo: *I play chess often*

c. Hago escalada raramente: *I go swimming rarely*

d. Cuando hace buen tiempo hago footing: *When the weather is nice I go hiking*

e. Voy en bici una vez a la semana: *I go biking every day*

f. Casi nunca juego al ajedrez: *I never play chess*

g. Hago senderismo a menudo: *I never go hiking*

h. Hago natación a menudo: *I go swimming from time to time*

THE LANGUAGE GYM

Unit 14. Free time: READING

Me llamo Thomas Weidner. Soy alemán. En mi tiempo libre hago mucho deporte. Mi deporte favorito es la escalada. Hago escalada todos los días. Cuando hace mal tiempo me quedo en casa *[I stay at home]* y juego al ajedrez o a las cartas. También me gusta mucho jugar con los videojuegos o a la Play. Juego a la Play a menudo.

Me llamo Verónica Palacín. Soy española, de Barbastro. Soy pelirroja y muy simpática y graciosa, pero no soy muy deportista. Prefiero leer libros *[read books]*, jugar con los videojuegos o al ajedrez y escuchar música. Cuando hace buen tiempo, sin embargo, a veces hago footing en el parque de mi barrio o juego al tenis con mi hermano. No me gusta ir al gimnasio ni a la piscina. Odio la natación porque no me gusta el agua.

Me llamo Olga. Soy de Chipre *(Cyprus)*. En mi tiempo libre me gusta mucho leer libros y periódicos. También me gusta jugar a las cartas y al ajedrez. No soy muy deportista. Pero, a veces voy al gimnasio y hago pesas. Además, en el fin de semana, cuando hace buen tiempo, hago senderismo en el campo con mi perro. Buddy es un perro salchicha y es pequeño y marrón.

Me llamo Ronan. Soy francés. Me encanta ir en bici. Voy en bici todos los días con mis amigos. Es mi deporte favorito. A veces hago escalada, footing o senderismo. No me gusta el tenis ni el fútbol. También odio hacer natación. Hago natación muy raramente. Dos veces por semana voy de marcha con mi amigo, Julien Barrett. Me encanta bailar.

1. Find the Spanish for the following in Thomas' text

a. I do a lot of sport

b. My favourite sport

c. Climbing

d. Every day

e. When the weather's bad

f. I play chess

g. Also

h. I play on the Playstation

2. Find the Spanish in Ronan's text for

a. I love biking

b. with my friends

c. sometimes

d. I do swimming

e. I go clubbing

f. I go rock climbing

g. with my friend, Julien

3. Complete the following statements about Verónica

a. She is from _____

b. She is not very _____

c. She plays videogames and _____

d. When the weather is nice she goes _____

e. She also plays tennis with her_____

f. She doesn't enjoy the gym nor the _____

4. List 8 details about Olga

1.

2.

3.

4.

5.

6.

7.

8.

5. Find Someone Who...

a. ...enjoys reading newspapers

b. ...hates swimming

c. ...does a lot of sport

d. ...does weight lifting

e. ...goes clubbing twice a week

Unit 14. Free time: TRANSLATION

1. Gapped translation

a. **Nunca voy de marcha:** _I _____ go clubbing_

b. **Juego a la Play a menudo:** _I often play _____

c. **No juego al tenis casi nunca:** _I _____ _____ play tennis_

d. **Juego al _____:** _I play chess_

e. **Juego a las _____:** _I play cards_

f. **A veces voy en bici:** _____, _I go cycling_

g. **Nunca hago pesas:** _I never do _____

h. **Cuando hace _____ tiempo hago footing:** _when the weather is nice, I go jogging_

2. Translate to English

a. Casi nunca

b. A veces

c. Cuando hace mal tiempo

d. A la casa de mi amigo

e. Nunca

f. Todos los días

g. Hago escalada

h. Voy de marcha

i. Voy de pesca

3. Translate into English

a. Nunca voy de pesca con mi padre

b. Juego a las cartas con mi hermano

c. Hago senderismo con mi madre

d. Juego al ajedrez con mi mejor amigo

e. Casi nunca juego a la Play con mi hermano

f. Voy a la discoteca todos los sábados

4. Translate into Spanish

a. _Bike_: B

b. _Rock climbing_: E

c. _Basketball_: B

d. _Fishing_: P

e. _Weights_: P

f. _Videogames_: V

g. _Chess_: A

h. _Cards_: C

i. _Hiking_: S

j. _Jogging_: F

5. Translate into Spanish

a. I 'do' jogging

b. I play chess

c. I 'do' rock climbing

d. I 'do' swimming

e. I 'do' horse riding

f. I do weights

g. I go clubbing

h. I play videogames

i. I 'do' cycling

j. I 'do' hiking

Unit 14. Free time: WRITING

1. Split sentences

Nunca	el parque
Juego al ajedrez a	deporte
Voy a la casa	hago escalada
Hago footing en	menudo
Juego a las	bici
Hago mucho	de mi amigo Paco
Voy en	gimnasio
Hago pesas en el	cartas

2. Complete the sentences

a. Nunca _____ footing

b. A veces _____ al ajedrez

c. _____ escalada de vez en cuando

d. _____ equitación a menudo

e. Juego al tenis _____ _____ días

f. Voy a _____ de mi amigo

g. En mi _____ libre

h. Hago _____ en el gimnasio

i. Hago _____ deberes

3. Spot and correct mistakes
(note: in some cases a word is missing)

a. Juego tenis:

b. Juego a las ajedrez:

c. Voy a casa mi amigo:

d. Casi nunca voy de bici:

e. Voy mis deberes:

f. Voy natación:

g. Hago pesos:

4. Complete the words

a. Aje_____

b. Balon_____

c. Sende_____

d. Video_____

e. Equi_____

f. Nun_____

g. A men_____

5. Write a paragraph for each of the people below in the first person singular (I):

Name	Sport I do	How often	Who with	Where	Why I like it
Juanita	Hiking	Every day	With my boyfriend	In the countryside	It's fun
Dylan	Weight-lifting	Often	With my friend James	At home	It's healthy
Alejo	Jogging	When the weather is nice	Alone	In the park	It's relaxing

THE LANGUAGE GYM

Grammar Time 12: Jugar, Hacer and Ir (Part 1)

Jugar *to play*		
juego *I play*	al ajedrez *chess*	
juegas *you play*	al baloncesto *basketball*	
juega *she/he plays*	a las cartas *cards*	
jugamos *we play*	al fútbol *football*	**a menudo** *often*
jugáis *you guys play*	al tenis *tennis*	
juegan *they play*	con mis amigos *with my friends*	
Hacer *to do*		**a veces** *sometimes*
hago *I do*	ciclismo *cycling*	
	deporte *sport*	
haces	equitación *horse riding*	
hace	escalada *rock climbing*	**casi nunca** *hardly ever*
hacemos	footing *jogging*	
hacéis	natación *swimming*	
hacen	los deberes *hw*	**dos veces por semana** *twice a week*
	pesas *weights*	
Ir *to go*		
	a casa de mi amigo/a *to my friend's house*	**raramente** *rarely*
voy *I go*	a la montaña *to the mountain*	
vas	a la piscina *to the pool*	
va	a la playa *to the beach*	
vamos	al gimnasio *to the gym*	**todos los días** *every day*
vais	al parque *to the park*	
van	de marcha *clubbing*	
	de pesca *fishing*	
	en bici *on a bike ride*	

1. Match

Hago	He/she does
Haces	We do
Hace	You do
Hacemos	I do
Hacéis	They do
Hacen	You guys do

2. Complete with the correct ending

a. (yo) Nunca hag___ mis deberes

b. Mi padre jueg___ al fútbol a menudo

c. ¿Qué deporte hace___ tú?

d. (nosotros) Nunca jug_____ al tenis

e. (vosotros) ¿Qué hac____ hoy?

f. Mis hermanos siempre jueg___ a la Play

g. (yo) Nunca jueg___ con los videojuegos

h. Mi hermano mayor hac___ artes marciales

i. Mis hermanos no jueg___ al ajedrez

j. Mi madre y yo jug_____ a las cartas

3. Write the correct form of JUGAR (to play)

a. I play: _____

b. You play: _____

c. She plays: _____

d. We play: _____

e. You guys play: _____

f. They play: _____

g. My brothers play: _____

h. You and I play: _____

i. He and I play: _____

4. Complete with the first person of HACER, IR or JUGAR: *hago, voy, juego*

a. Nunca _____ al baloncesto

b. _____ deporte todos los días

c. _____ al voleibol

d. _____ a las cartas raramente

e. Nunca _____ ciclismo

f. _____ a la Play todos los días

g. _____ de pesca muy raramente

h. _____ escalada a menudo

i. _____ al estadio con mi padre

5. Spot and correct the translation errors

a. Voy de pesca *You go fishing*

b. Vas a la iglesia *You go to the igloo*

c. Vamos al centro comercial
You guys go to the shopping mall

d. Nunca voy a casa de Marta
We never go to Marta's house

e. Van al cine una vez por semana
She goes to the cinema once a week

6. Complete the forms of IR below

a. V_ _ de pesca   *I go fishing*

b. V_ _ al parque   *They go to the park*

c. V_ _ _ _ _ a la playa   *We go to the beach*

d. V_ _ a la piscina   *They go to the swimming pool*

e. ¿Adónde v_ _ _ ?   *Where are you going?*

 **THE LANGUAGE GYM**

7. Complete with *hace, juega* or *va* as appropriate

a. Mi madre nunca _____ deporte

b. Mi padre _____ a la iglesia raramente

c. Mi hermano _____ a la mezquita todos los viernes

d. Mi abuelo nunca _____ a las cartas conmigo

e. Mi hermano mayor _____ artes marciales

f. Mi amigo Paco siempre _____ a la Play

g. Mi hermano menor _____ ciclismo a menudo

h. Mi abuela _____ a la playa todos los días

8. Complete with *hacen, juegan* or *van* as appropriate

a. Mis padres nunca _____ al baloncesto

b. Mis hermanos no _____ deporte

c. Mis hermanos nunca _____ al fútbol

d. Mi madre y mi padre _____ a las cartas

e. Mis primos _____ artes marciales

f. Ellas _____ de pesca a menudo

g. Mis tíos _____ a la iglesia muy raramente

h. Mis amigos nunca _____ escalada conmigo

i. ¿Tus amigos _____ ciclismo?

j. Mis amigos, Mok y Laura, _____ al ajedrez

k. Ellos _____ a la piscina

9. Translate into English

a. Nunca juego al fútbol

b. Hace sus deberes a menudo

c. Nunca vamos a la iglesia

d. No van a la piscina a menudo

e. Cuando hace buen tiempo van al parque

f. Nunca juego al ajedrez

g. Cuando hace mal tiempo voy al gimnasio

10. Translate into Spanish

a. We never go to the swimming pool

b. They do sport rarely

c. She plays basketball every day

d. When the weather is nice, I do jogging

e. I rarely do cycling

f. I do rock climbing often

g. My father and I often play badminton

h. My sister plays tennis twice a week

i. I go to the swimming pool on Saturdays

j. When the weather is bad I go to the gym

k. They rarely do their homework

l. We never play chess

UNIT 15
Talking about weather and free time

GRAMMAR TIME: Jugar / Hacer / Ir
Question skills: Clothes / Free time / Weather

In this unit you will learn how to say:
- What free-time activities you do in different types of Weather
- Where you do them **and** who with
- Words for places in town

You will also learn how to ask and answer questions about:
- Clothes
- Free time
- Weather

You will revisit:
- Sports and hobbies
- The verbs 'hacer', 'ir' and 'jugar' in the present indicative
- Pets
- Places in town
- Clothes
- Family members
- Numbers from 1 to 100

Unit 15
Talking about weather and free time

A veces *Sometimes* **Entre semana** *On weekdays* **Los fines de semana** *At the weekends* **Cuando tengo tiempo** *When I have time* **Cuando está despejado** *When the sky is clear* **Cuando está nublado** *When the sky is cloudy* **Cuando hace buen tiempo** *When the weather is good* **Cuando hace mal tiempo** *When the weather is bad* **Cuando hace calor** *When it is hot* **Cuando hace frío** *When it is cold* **Cuando hace sol** *When it is sunny* **Cuando hace viento** *When it is windy* **Cuando hay niebla** *When it is foggy* **Cuando hay tormentas** *When there are storms* **Cuando llueve** *When it rains* **Cuando nieva** *When it snows*	**juego** *I play* **mi amiga María juega** *my friend Maria plays*	**al ajedrez** *chess* **a las cartas** *cards* **al baloncesto** *basketball* **al fútbol** *football* **al tenis** *tennis* **con mis amigos** *with my friends* **con sus amigos** *with his/her friends*
	hago *I do* **mi amigo Lionel hace** *my friend Lionel does*	**ciclismo** *cycling* **deporte** *sport* **equitación** *horse riding* **escalada** *rock climbing* **esquí** *skiing* **footing** *jogging* **natación** *swimming* **los deberes** *hw* **senderismo** *hiking*
	voy *I go* **mi amigo va** *my friend (m) goes* **mi amiga va** *my friend (f) goes*	**a casa de mi amigo** *to my friend's house* **a casa de su amigo** *to his/her friend's house* **al campo** *to the countryside* **al centro comercial** *to the mall* **al gimnasio** *to the gym* **a la montaña** *to the mountain* **al parque** *to the park* **a la piscina** *to the pool* **a la playa** *to the beach* **al polideportivo** *to the sports centre* **de marcha** *clubbing* **de pesca** *fishing* **en bici** *on a bike ride*
	me quedo *I stay*	**en mi casa** *in my home* **en mi habitación** *in my room*
	Felipe María **se queda** *stays*	**en su casa** *in his/her home* **en su habitación** *in his/her room*

Unit 15. Talking about weather and free time VOCABULARY BUILDING 1

1. Match up

Cuando	It's cold
Hace frío	It's hot
Hace calor	It's clear skies
Hace buen tiempo	When
Hace mal tiempo	It's good weather
Está despejado	It's raining
Llueve	It's bad weather

2. Translate into English

a. Cuando hace frío

b. Cuando llueve

c. Está despejado

d. Cuando hace calor

e. Cuando nieva

f. Cuando hace buen tiempo

g. Cuando hay niebla

h. Juego al tenis

i. Hago esquí

j. Cuando hace mal tiempo

3. Complete with the missing word

a. Cuando hace_____ tiempo
When it's bad weather

b. Cuando _____y hace _____
When it rains and is cold

c. Cuando _____ sol y hace _____
When it is sunny and hot

d. Cuando hay tormentas me _____en casa
When it is stormy I stay at home

e. Cuando hace_____ tiempo voy al parque
When it's good weather I go to the park

f. Cuando _____ hago esquí en la montaña
When it snows I ski on the mountain

g. Cuando hace mal _____ mi amigo se queda en su
casa *When the weather is bad my friend stays at home*

h. Me gusta cuando hace _____ *I like it when it's sunny*

4. Anagrams: weather

a. fíor	e. desadopej	i. yah blaine
b. orcal	f. lam tempoi	j. blanudo
c. nieav	g. ceha slo	k. toentasrm
d. luelve	h. vtoien	l. benu tpoime

5. Associations – match each weather word below with the clothes/activities in the box

a. Mal tiempo: tormentas, viento, lluvia –

b. Hace buen tiempo: sol y calor –

c. Nieva y hace frío –

botas de nieve	me quedo en casa	hago esquí	la playa
no hago nada	pantalón corto	veo la tele	sombrero
la montaña	bufanda	pijama	bañador

6. Complete

a. Hace buen _____ *It's good weather*

b. Me quedo en c_____ *I stay at home*

c. Cuando l_____ *When it rains*

d. Me _____ cuando hace calor
I like it when it's hot

e. _____ a la playa *I go to the beach*

f. Cuando _____ tormentas
When there are storms

g. Cuando _____ despejado
When the skies are clear

h. Cuando está _____
When it is cloudy

Unit 15. Talking about weather and free time: VOCABULARY BUILDING 2

1. Match up

Juego al tenis	I go clubbing
Juego a las cartas	In his bedroom
Hago equitación	She goes fishing
Voy de marcha	I play tennis
Ella va de pesca	I do horseriding
En su dormitorio	I play cards
Me quedo en casa	Swimming
La natación	I stay at home

3. Translate into English

a. La casa de mi amigo

b. Hago equitación

c. Está despejado

d. Hago escalada

e. Hace footing

f. Va al polideportivo

g. Voy a la piscina

h. Hago deporte

2. Complete with the missing word

a. Me quedo en _____ habitación *I stay in my bedroom*

b. Mi amigo _____ a la playa *My friend goes to the beach*

c. Voy a _____ de mi _____ *I go to my friend's house*

d. Voy al _____ *I go to the sports centre*

e. _____ semana siempre hago mis deberes
I always do my homework on weekdays

f. Me gustan los fines de _____ *I like the weekends*

g. Juego con mis _____ *I play with my friends*

h. Mi amiga Vero siempre _____ a casa de ___ amigo
My friend Vero always goes to her friend's house

i. Siempre hago _____ *I always do hiking*

4. Anagrams: activities

a. foinotg

b. naciatón

c. sendsmerio

d. equtiacinó

e. bonalcesto

f. búftol

g. tracas

h. ajeezdr

i. cernto corcmeial

j. de chamra

k. de pecsa

l. poderte

5. Broken words

a. J_____ a___f_____ c_____ mis a_____s
I play football with my friends

b. M_ t_____ M_____ j_____ a l___ c_____
My aunt Maria plays cards

c. V_____ a c___ d__ m_ a_____
I go to my friend's house

d. J_____ v_ a_ p_____
Joaquín goes to the sports centre

e. H_____ e_____ c____m___ c_____
I do horse riding with my horse

f. M__ a_____ s__ q_____ e__ c_____ y h_____ l____
d_____ *My friend stays at home and does homework*

6. Complete

a. Hago los _____ *I do homework*

b. Se _____ en casa
He stays at home

c. Hace _____ *He does swimming*

d. Voy ___ gimnasio *I go to the gym*

e. _____ a la piscina *I go to the pool*

f. Me quedo en _____ *I stay home*

g. Hago _____ *I do climbing*

h. Hago _____ en la _____
I do skiing in the mountain

i. En mi _____ *in my room*

Unit 15. Talking about weather and free time: READING

Me llamo Pietro. Soy de Italia. Tengo once años. Soy muy deportista, entonces me gusta cuando hace buen tiempo. Cuando hace sol siempre voy al parque con mis amigos y juego al fútbol. También, cuando hace calor siempre voy a la playa con mi perro. Es pequeño y negro, y muy simpático. Yo llevo un bañador, sandalias y un sombrero cuando voy a la playa.

Me llamo Isabela. Soy de Roma, en Italia. Tengo quince años. Me encanta comprar camisetas y chaquetas. Me encanta cuando hay tormentas. Me quedo en casa con mi hermano mayor y juego a videojuegos o a las cartas con él. Las tormentas son muy bonitas y divertidas. No me gusta cuando hace frío porque no me gusta llevar abrigos y bufandas. ¡En casa tengo un perro, un gato y un loro que habla italiano!

Me llamo Ana Laura. Soy de Brasil. Tengo doce años. Me encanta cantar en mi tiempo libre. Cuando hace frío voy al centro comercial con mis amigas. Llevo un abrigo, una bufanda y unas botas. ¡Me encanta el frío! Mi película favorita es Frozen 2. Cuando hace calor me quedo en casa porque no me gusta. Nunca voy a la playa. ¡Odio la playa!

Me llamo Chloé. Soy de Francia. Tengo catorce años. Cuando hace calor y está despejado voy a la piscina y hago natación. También voy de pesca con mi padre en su barco. Es un poco aburrido pero me gusta de todas formas. Por la noche voy de marcha con mis amigos. Cuando voy a la discoteca por lo general llevo una camiseta y vaqueros. Mi amiga se llama Sofía. Es simpática e inteligente. Si hace mal tiempo y llueve ella siempre se queda en su casa y hace sus deberes.

1. Find the Spanish for the following in Pietro's text

a. I am from

b. I am 11

c. I like it

d. when

e. it is sunny

f. I go to the park

g. with my dog

h. small and black

i. a swimsuit

j. the beach

2. Find the Spanish for the following in Chloe's text

a. when it's hot

b. it's clear

c. I swim

d. I go fishing

e. a bit boring

f. I go clubbing

g. a t-shirt

h. is called

i. stays

j. in her house

3. Complete the following statements about Isabela

a. She is _____ years old

b. She loves buying _____ and _____

c. She loves it when there are _____

d. When it's stormy she plays _____ or _____ with her _____ brother

e. Isabela does not like _____weather

f. Her pet can _____ Italian

4. Answer in Spanish the questions below about Ana Laura

a. ¿De dónde es?

b. ¿Cuántos años tiene?

c. ¿Qué hace en su tiempo libre?

d. ¿Qué tiempo le gusta?

e. ¿Adónde va cuando hace frío?

f. ¿Qué hace cuando hace calor?

g. ¿Le gusta el calor?

h. ¿Cuál es su película favorita?

5. Find Someone Who...

a. ...likes to go fishing
b. ...is from france
c. ...loves really cold weather
d. ...has three pets at home
e. ...thinks that storms are pretty
f. ...wears jeans to go out
g. ...goes to the beach with an animal
h. ...never goes to the beach
i. ...owns a boat

Unit 15. Talking about weather and free time: WRITING

1. Split sentences

Me gusta cuando	sol voy a la playa
No me	un abrigo y una bufanda
Cuando hace	hace frío
Cuando hace mucho frío llevo	gusta la lluvia
Las tormentas son	hago esquí
Cuando hace mal tiempo	me quedo en casa
Cuando hace buen	muy bonitas
Cuando nieva	tiempo voy al parque

2. Complete with the correct option

a. _____ hace frío llevo una bufanda. ¡No me _____!

b. _____ semana hago los deberes.

c. Cuando _____ mal tiempo me _____ en casa.

d. Cuando _____ niebla no voy a la _____

e. Cuando hace _____ voy a la playa

f. Cuando _____ despejado hago senderismo en el campo

g. Cuando hace mal tiempo mi amigo Pepe se queda en _____ casa

calor	hay	quedo	montaña	entre
gusta	hace	cuando	está	su

3. Spot and correct the grammar and spelling mistakes note: in several cases a word is missing

a. Cuando hace viento voy a la gimnasio con mi amigo

b. Cuando esta nublado mi amiga Juana juega al tenis

c. Me encantan la tormentas, son muy bonita

d. Cuando hace malo tiempo mi amigo me queda en casa

e. Cuando hace niebla no juego al baloncesto

f. Los fins de semana voy ala playa con mi perro

g. Cuando hace sol voy al campo, lleva una camiseta blanco

h. (yo) Siempre lleva zapatillos de deporte cuando juego al fútbol

4. Complete the words

a. F_____   *cold*

b. C_____   *hot*

c. N_____   *cloudy*

d. C_____   *when*

e. T_____   *storms*

f. V_____   *wind*

g. N_____   *fog*

6. Describe this person in Spanish using the 3rd person she

Name: Paula

Lives in: Mérida

Age : 13

Pet: A white dog

Weather: Sunny and good weather

Always: Goes to the countryside and does hiking

Never: Stays at home and does homework

5. Guided writing – write 3 short paragraphs in the first person I using the details below

Person	Lives	Weather	Activity	With
Elías	Sevilla	Good weather	Go to the park	Friends
Santino	Córdoba	Hot and sunny	Go to the beach	Dog
Julieta	Huelva /welva/	Cold and rainy	Stay home	Older sister

Grammar Time 13: Jugar, Hacer, Ir + Ser and Tener

Jugar to play		
*(yo) juego *I play* (tú) juegas *you...* (él) juega *he...* (ella) juega *she...*	(nosotros) jugamos *we play...* (vosotros) jugáis *you guys ...* (ellos) juegan *they... masc/**mixed* (ellos) juegan *they... all female*	al ajedrez al baloncesto a las cartas con mis amigos/amigas

Hacer to do			
hago haces hace	hacemos hacéis hacen	deporte footing los deberes	natación pesas *(weights)*

Ir to go			
voy vas va	vamos vais van	a la piscina de pesca en bici	al gimnasio al parque

Ser to be

		Masc. sing	Fem. sing	Masc. plural	Fem. plural
soy	somos	alto	alta	altos	altas
eres	sois	guapo	guapa	guapos	guapas
es	son	francés	francesa	franceses	francesas
		alemán	alemana	alemanes	alemanas

Tener to have			
tengo tienes tiene	tenemos tenéis tienen	dos hermanos los ojos negros el pelo castaño	once años un perro y un gato

*Author's note: the subject pronouns "yo", "tú", "él", "ella", "nosotros", "vosotros", "ellos", "ellas" are OPTIONAL, not obligatory. They are useful to:

1) Add emphasis
2) Help know who we are talking about in the third person (he/she)

**"Ellos" means "they" and should be used for a group of males AND/OR a mixed group of males and females.

 THE LANGUAGE GYM

1. Complete with the one of the following verbs: *Tengo – Voy – Soy – Juego – Hago*

a. _____ deporte

b. _____ al parque

c. _____ un gato

d. _____ al fútbol

e. _____ a las cartas

f. _____ un perro

g. _____ quince años

h. _____ dos mascotas

i. _____ al cine

j. _____ escalada

k. _____ ciclismo

l. _____ al ajedrez

m. _____ al baloncesto

n. _____ los ojos negros

o. _____ el pelo rubio

2. Rewrite the sentences in the first column in the third person singular

yo	él , ella
juego al tenis	
voy al cine	
tengo un gato	
soy alta	
hago natación	

4. Complete

a. Yo nunca v_____ a la piscina

b. Mi madre nunca v_____ a la iglesia

c. (nosotros) v_____ a la iglesia a menudo

d. Mi hermano t_____ un gato

e. Ellos s_____ ingleses, yo s_____ italiano

f. Mis padres t_____ el pelo pelirrojo

g. Mi hermano y yo _____ artes marciales

5. Complete with the appropriate verb

a. (yo) nunca _____ al cine con mis padres

b. Mi hermana y yo _____ al parque

c. Mi madre _____ cuarenta años

d. Mi primo _____ muy alto y guapo

e. Mis hermanos _____ a la Play a menudo

f. (él) Nunca _____ deporte

g. Cuando hace buen tiempo (él) _____ a la playa

3. Translate into English

a. Hacemos natación

b. Jugamos al ajedrez

c. No hacen nada

d. Van al cine

e. Tenemos dos perros

f. Somos franceses

g. No tiene hermanos

h. No soy de Madrid

i. No hago nada

6. Translate into Spanish

a. I never play tennis with him

b. My mother never goes to church

c. My brother is tall and slim. He has blond hair and blue eyes

d. My father is forty years old

e. My brother goes to the gym every day

f. They never go to the swimming pool

Revision Quickie 4: Clothes/Free time/Weather

1. Activities - Match

Hago los deberes	I go to church
Hago deporte	I go to the swimming pool
Juego al baloncesto	I go to the gym
Juego a las cartas	I go window shopping
Voy a la iglesia	I do the homework
Voy a la piscina	I go swimming
Voy al gimnasio	I do rock climbing
Miro escaparates	I do sport
Hago natación	I go horse-riding
Hago equitación	I go to the beach
Voy a la playa	I play cards
Hago escalada	I play basketball

2. Weather – Complete

a. Hace fr_ _

b. Hace ca_ _ _

c. Hace s_ _

d. Hay ni_ _ _ _ _

e. Hace bu_ _ t_ _ _ _ _ _

f. Hace ma_ t_ _ _ _ _ _

g. Hay to_ _ _ _ _ _ _ _

h. Hace vi_ _ _ _ _

i. Ll_ _ _ _ _

3. Fill in the gaps in Spanish

a. Cuando hace f_____, llevo un a_____   *When it is cold I wear a coat*

b. Cuando hace m_____ t_____, me q_____ en casa   *When the weather is bad I stay at home*

c. Cuando h_____ s_____ voy a la p_____   *When it is sunny I go to the beach*

d. Cuando v_____ al gimnasio, l_____ un c_____   *When I go to the gym I wear a tracksuit*

e. Cuando hace c_____, voy a l__ p_____   *When it is hot I go to the swimming pool*

f. En el fin de semana h_____ m_____ d_____   *At the week-end I do my homework*

g. Cuando t_____ t_____ l_____   *When I have free time*

h. H_____ e_____   *I go rock climbing*

4. Translate into Spanish

a. When it is hot:

b. When it is cold:

c. I play basketball:

d. I do my homework:

e. I go rock climbing:

f. When I have free time:

g. I go to the swimming-pool:

h. I go to the gym:

5. Translate to Spanish

a. I wear a coat

b. We wear a uniform

c. They play basketball

d. She goes rock climbing

e. He has free time

f. They go swimming

g. My parents do sport

h. She plays football often

Question Skills 3: Clothes/Free time/Weather

1. Translate into English

a. ¿Qué ropa llevas cuando hace frío?

b. ¿Qué tiempo hace donde vives?

c. ¿Qué haces en tu tiempo libre?

d. ¿Haces deporte?

e. ¿Con qué frecuencia juegas al baloncesto?

f. ¿Por qué no te gusta el fútbol?

g. ¿Dónde haces escalada?

h. ¿Cuál es tu deporte preferido?

2. Complete with the missing question word:

a. ¿_____ vives?

b. ¿_____ deporte haces?

c. ¿ _____ deporte prefieres?

d. ¿_____ haces natación?

e. ¿_____ compras tus zapatos?

f. ¿_____ te gusta hacer en tu tiempo libre?

g. ¿Con _____ juegas al tenis?

h. ¿Con _____ frecuencia haces equitación?

i. ¿ _____ _____ no juegas conmigo? :(

3. Split questions

¿Qué haces	escalada?
¿Con quién	haces cuando hace frío?
¿Por	en tu tiempo libre?
¿Dónde haces	ropa nueva?
¿Qué	juegas al ajedrez?
¿Cuál es	cuando hace calor?
¿Tienes mucha	tu deporte preferido?
¿Qué ropa llevas	qué no te gusta el tenis?

4. Translate into Spanish

a. What?

b. Where?

c. How?

d. When?

e. Why?

f. How much? (m. sg)

g. How many? (f. pl)

h. From where?

i. Which?

5. Write the questions to these answers

a. Cuando hace frío llevo un abrigo

b. En el fin de semana hago deporte

c. Voy al gimnasio a las cinco de la tarde

d. Tengo dos chándales

e. Juego al tenis con mi padre o mi hermano

f. Hago natación en la piscina cerca de mi casa

g. Hago escalada raramente

6. Translate into Spanish

a. Where do you play tennis?

b. What do you do when you have free time?

c. How many shoes do you have?

d. What is your favourite hobby?

e. Do you do sport often?

f. At what time do you do your homework?

THE LANGUAGE GYM

UNIT 16
Talking about my
daily routine

In this unit you will learn how to say:

- What you do every day
- At what time you do it
- Sequencing events/actions (e.g. using 'then', 'finally')

You will revisit:
- Numbers
- Free time activities
- Nationalities
- Clothes
- Hair and eyes
- Food
- Jobs

UNIT 16
Talking about my daily routine

A eso de... At *around...*	**de la mañana** *in the morning*	**almuerzo** *I have lunch*	**luego...** *then*
A... *At*		**ceno** *I have dinner*	
...la una *1*			**después...** *after*
...las cinco *5*	**de la tarde** *in the evening*	**desayuno** *I have breakfast*	
...las seis *6*		**descanso** *I rest*	**finalmente...** *finally*
...las siete *7*			
...las ocho y cinco *8.05*		**hago mis deberes** *I do my homework*	
...las ocho y diez *8.10*	**de la noche** *at night*		
...las ocho y cuarto *8.15*		**juego en el ordenador** *I play on the computer*	
...las ocho y veinte *8.20*			
...las ocho y veinticinco *8.25*		**me acuesto** *I go to bed*	
...las ocho y media *8.30*		**me lavo los dientes** *I brush my teeth*	
...las ocho y treinta y cinco *8.35*			
...las nueve menos veinte *8.40*		**me levanto** *I get up*	
...las nueve menos cuarto *8.45*		**me visto** *I get dressed*	
...las nueve menos diez *8.50*			
...las nueve menos cinco *8.55*		**salgo de casa** *I leave my house*	
A mediodía *12 pm*		**voy al colegio en autobús** *I go to school by bus*	
A medianoche *12 am*			
		veo la tele *I watch television*	
		vuelvo a casa *I go back home*	

> **Author's Note:** a "la una" is the only time which has "la". Watch out for it!

Unit 16. Talking about my daily routine: VOCAB BUILDING (Part 1)

1. Match up

Me levanto	I have lunch
Voy al colegio	I have dinner
Me acuesto	I get up
Almuerzo	I have breakfast
Ceno	I rest
Desayuno	I go to school
Descanso	I go back home
Vuelvo a casa	I go to bed

2. Translate into English

a. Me levanto a las seis de la mañana

b. Me acuesto a las once de la noche

c. Almuerzo a mediodía

d. Desayuno a las seis de la mañana

e. Vuelvo a casa a las tres y media de la tarde

f. Ceno a eso de las ocho de la tarde

g. Veo la tele

h. Escucho música

i. Salgo de casa a las siete de la mañana

3. Complete with the missing words

a. _____ al colegio   *I go to school*

b. _____ de casa   *I leave the house*

c. _____ a casa   *I come back home*

d. _____ la tele   *I watch television*

e. _____ mis deberes   *I do my homework*

f. _____ música   *I listen to music*

g. _____ en el ordenador   *I play on the computer*

h. _____ a mediodía   *I have lunch at noon*

4. Complete with the missing letters

a. ____escanso   *I rest*

b. ____uelvo a ___asa   *I go back home*

c. ____scucho música   *I listen to music*

d. ____esayuno   *I have breakfast*

e. ____eno   *I have dinner*

f. ____oy al colegio   *I go to school*

g. Me ____evanto   *I get up*

h. Me ____cuesto   *I go to bed*

i. ___lmuerzo   *I have lunch*

5. Faulty translation – spot and correct any translation mistakes. Not all translations are wrong.

a. Descanso un poco: *I shower a bit*

b. Me acuesto a medianoche: *I go to bed at noon*

c. Hago mis deberes: *I do your homework*

d. Almuerzo: *I have lunch*

e. Voy al colegio: *I come back from school*

f. Vuelvo a casa: *I leave the house*

g. Veo la tele: *I watch television*

h. Salgo de casa: *I leave school*

i. Me lavo los dientes: *I wash my hands*

6. Translate the following times into Spanish *(add de la mañana / tarde / noche where appropriate)*

a. At 6.30 a.m.

b. At 7.30 a.m.

c. At 8.20 p.m.

d. At midday

e. At 9.20 a.m.

f. At 11.00 p.m.

g. At midnight

h. At 5.15 p.m.

Unit 16. Talking about my daily routine: VOCAB BUILDING (Part 2)

1. Complete the table

Me acuesto	
	I brush my teeth
Me levanto	
	I go back home
A las ocho y cuarto	
Almuerzo	
	I have dinner
Escucho música	
	I leave the house
Desayuno	
Descanso	
	I do my homework
Me visto	

2. Complete the sentences using the words in the table

a. A las siete y _____   *At seven thirty*

b. A _____ de las cinco   *At about 5.00*

c. A las ocho de la _____   *At 8.00 a.m.*

d. A _____   *At noon*

e. A las _____ y cuarto   *At 11.15*

f. A las tres _____ veinte   *At 2.40*

g. A _____   *At midnight*

h. A eso de _____ cuatro   *At about 4.00*

i. _____ eso de las siete   *At about 7.00*

j. A las ocho menos _____   *At 7.55*

cinco	media	las	mañana	mediodía
once	a	menos	eso	medianoche

3. Translate into English (numerical)

a. A las ocho y media _____ ***At 8.30*** _____

b. A las nueve y cuarto _____

c. A las diez menos cinco _____

d. A mediodía _____

e. A medianoche _____

f. A las once menos cinco _____

g. A las doce y veinte _____

4. Complete

a. A l____ c_____ y m_____   *At 5.30*

b. A l___ o_____ y c_____   *At 8.15*

c. A m_____   *At noon*

d. A las o_____ m_____ c_____   *At 7.45*

e. A m_____   *At midnight*

f. A las o_____ y m_____   *At 11.30*

g. A e_____ d____ l___ u_____   *At about 1.00*

5. Translate the following into Spanish

a. I go to school at around 8

b. I come back home at around 3

c. I have dinner at 7.30

d. I do my homework at around 5.30

e. I have breakfast at 6.45

f. I go to bed at midnight

g. I have lunch at midday

Unit 16. Talking about my daily routine: READING (Part 1)

Me llamo Hiroto. Soy Japonés. Mi rutina diaria es muy sencilla. Por lo general, me levanto a eso de las seis. Luego me ducho y me visto. Después, desayuno con mi padre y mi hermano menor. Luego me lavo los dientes y me peino. A eso de las siete y media salgo de casa y voy al colegio. Voy en bici. Vuelvo a casa a eso de las cuatro. Luego descanso un poco. Por lo general veo la tele. Entonces, voy al parque con mis amigos hasta las seis. Desde las seis hasta las siete y media hago mis deberes. Luego, a las ocho, ceno con mi familia. No como mucho. Solo una hamburguesa. Después, veo una película en la tele y, a eso de las once, me acuesto.

Me llamo Gregorio. Soy mexicano. Mi rutina diaria es muy simple. Por lo general, me levanto a las seis y cuarto. Luego me ducho y desayuno con mis dos hermanos. Después, me lavo los dientes y preparo mi mochila. A eso de las siete voy al colegio. Voy al colegio a pie. Vuelvo a casa a eso de las tres y media. Luego me relajo un poco. Por lo general navego por internet, veo una serie en Netflix o chateo con mis amigos en Whatsapp o Snapchat. Desde las cinco hasta las seis, hago mis deberes. Luego, a las siete y media, ceno con mi familia. Como arroz o ensalada. Después, veo la tele y, a eso de las once y media, me acuesto.

Me llamo Andreas. Soy alemán. Mi rutina diaria es muy sencilla. Por lo general, me levanto temprano, a eso de las cinco. Hago footing y luego me ducho y me visto. Después, a eso de las seis y media, desayuno fruta con mi madre y mi hermana. Luego me lavo los dientes y preparo mi mochila. A eso de las siete y cuarto salgo de casa y voy al colegio. Vuelvo a casa a eso de las tres y media. Luego, descanso un poco. Por lo general, veo la tele o chateo con mis amigos en internet. Desde las seis hasta las ocho hago mis deberes. Luego, a las ocho y cuarto, ceno con mi familia. No como mucho. Después, juego a la Play hasta medianoche. Finalmente, me acuesto.

1. Answer the following questions about Hiroto

a. Where is he from?

b. At what time does he get up?

c. Who does he have breakfast with?

d. At what time does he leave the house?

e. Until what time does he stay at the park?

f. How does he go to school?

2. Find the Spanish for the phrases below in Hiroto's text

a. At around eleven

b. With my friends

c. I go by bike

d. I go to the park

e. I shower and get dressed

f. I don't eat much

g. From six to seven

h. I do my homework

3. Complete the statements below about Andreas

a. He gets up at _____

b. He comes back from school at _____

c. For breakfast he eats _____

d. He has breakfast with _____

e. After getting up he _____ and then showers

f. Usually he _____ until midnight

g. After breakfast he brushes his teeth and then

_____.

4. Find the Spanish for the following phrases/sentences in Gregorio's text

a. I am Mexican

b. I shower

c. With my two brothers

d. I relax a bit

e. I eat rice or salad

f. I surf the internet

g. I have dinner

Unit 16. Talking about my daily routine: READING (Part 2)

Me llamo Yang. Tengo doce años. Soy chino. Mi rutina diaria es muy sencilla. Por lo general, me levanto a eso de las seis y media. Luego me ducho y me visto. Después, desayuno con mi madre y mi hermano, Li Wei. Luego me lavo los dientes y preparo mi mochila. A eso de las siete y media salgo de casa y voy al colegio. Vuelvo a casa a eso de las cuatro. Luego descanso un poco. Por lo general veo la tele, escucho música o leo mis tebeos preferidos. Desde las seis hasta las siete y media hago mis deberes. Luego, a las ocho, ceno con mi familia. No como mucho. Después, veo una película en la tele y, a eso de las once, me acuesto.

Me llamo Anna. Soy italiana. Mi rutina diaria es muy sencilla. Por lo general, me levanto a las seis y cuarto. Luego me lavo y desayuno con mi hermana mayor. Después, me lavo los dientes y preparo mi mochila. A eso de las siete voy al colegio en autobús. Vuelvo a casa a eso de las dos y media. Luego descanso un poco. Por lo general navego por internet, veo la tele o leo revistas de moda. Desde las cinco hasta las siete, hago mis deberes. Luego, a las ocho, ceno con mi familia. Como fruta o una ensalada. Después, leo una novela y, a eso de las once y media, me acuesto.

Me llamo Kim, soy inglesa. Tengo quince años. Mi rutina diaria es muy sencilla. Por lo general, me levanto temprano, a eso de las cinco y media. Hago ejercicio y luego me lavo y me visto. Después, a eso de las siete, desayuno con mi madre y mi hermanastra. Luego me lavo los dientes y preparo mi mochila. A eso de las siete y media salgo de casa y voy al colegio. Vuelvo a casa a eso de las tres. Luego, descanso un poco. Por lo general, escucho música o chateo con mis amigos en Internet. Desde las seis hasta las ocho hago mis deberes. Luego, a las ocho y cuarto, ceno con mi familia. Como bastante. Después, veo una película en la tele hasta medianoche. Finalmente, me acuesto.

1. Find the Spanish for the following in Yang's text

a. I am Chinese

b. My daily routine

c. I shower

d. Very simple

e. At around 7.30

f. I don't eat much

g. I watch television

h. I go to school

i. I do my homework

j. From six to seven

2. Translate these items from Kim's text

a. I am English

b. Generally

c. At around 5.30

d. With my mum and stepsister

e. I go back home

f. I have dinner with my family

g. I rest a bit

h. I brush my teeth

3. Answer the following questions on Anna's text

a. What nationality is Anna?

b. At what time does she get up?

c. What three things does she do after school?

d. How does she go to school?

e. Who does she have breakfast with?

f. At what time does she go to bed?

g. What does she eat for dinner?

h. What does she read before going to bed?

4. Find Someone Who...

a. ...has breakfast with their older sister

b. ...doesn't watch television at night

c. ...reads fashion magazines

d. ...gets up at 5.30am

e. ...has breakfast with their brother and mother

f. ...chats with their friends on the internet after school

g. ...does exercise in the morning

 THE LANGUAGE GYM

Unit 16. Talking about my daily routine: WRITING

1. Split sentences

Voy al colegio	casa
Vuelvo a	deberes
Hago mis	en autobús
Veo	la tele
Juego en el	a medianoche
Me levanto a	de casa
Me acuesto	eso de las seis
Salgo	ordenador

2. Complete with the correct option

a. Me levanto a _____ siete de la mañana

b. Hago _____ deberes

c. Veo _____ tele

d. Juego en el _____

e. Me _____ a medianoche

f. Vuelvo _____ casa

g. Salgo de _____

h. Voy al colegio _____ autobús

a	acuesto	las	en
la	mis	casa	ordenador

3. Spot and correct the grammar and spelling mistakes in several cases a word is missing

a. Voy a colegio en bici

b. Me levanto a la siete y media

c. Salgo casa a las ocho

d. Vuelvo al casa

e. Voy colegio en autobús

f. Me acuesto a eso las once

g. Ceno a las ocho meno cuarto

h. Hago mi deberes a las cinco media

4. Complete the words

a. cu_____ *quarter*

b. me_____ *half*

c. a l____ di____ *at 10*

d. a e_____ d__ *at around*

e. a l_____ o_____ *at 8*

f. ve_____ *twenty*

g. l_____ *then*

h. a_____ *I have lunch*

i. v_____ *I come back*

j. j_____ *I play*

5. Guided writing – write 3 short paragraphs in the first person I using the details below

Person	Gets up	Showers	Goes to school	Comes back home	Watches TV	Has dinner	Goes to bed
Elías	6.30	7.00	8.05	3.30	6.00	8.10	11.10
Santino	6.40	7.10	7.40	4.00	6.30	8.15	12.00
Julieta	7.15	7.30	8.00	3.15	6.40	8.20	11.30

THE LANGUAGE GYM

Revision Quickie 5: Clothes / Food / Free Time / Describing people

1. Clothes – Match up

Una bufanda (1)	A baseball cap
Un traje	A skirt
Una gorra	A dress
Una corbata	A shirt
Una falda	A T-shirt
Un vestido	Jeans
Una camiseta	A suit
Una camisa	Socks
Unos vaqueros	Trousers
Unos calcetines	A scarf (1)
Unos pantalones	A tie

3. Complete the translations below

a. Shoes: zap_____

b. Hat: som_____

c. Hair: pe_____

d. Curly: riz_____

e. Purple: mor_____

f. Milk: le_____

g. Water: ag_____

h. Drink: be_____

i. Job: tr_____

k. Clothes: ro_____

5. Match questions and answers

¿Cuál es tu trabajo preferido?	Un chándal
¿Qué color te gusta más?	El de dibujo
¿Qué carne no te gusta?	El de abogado
¿Qué llevas por lo general en el gimnasio?	El ajedrez
¿Cuál es tu profe preferido?	El azul
¿Cuál es tu bebida preferida?	El cerdo
¿Cuál es tu pasatiempo preferido?	El zumo de fruta

2. Food – Provide a word for each of the cues below

A fruit starting with **M**	la manzana
A vegetable starting with **Z**	
A dairy product starting with **Q**	
A meat starting with **C**	
A drink starting with **Z**	
A drink made using lemons **L**	
A sweet dessert starting with **P**	
A fruit starting with **C**	

4. Clothes, Colours, Food, Jobs – Categories

Ropa	Colores	Trabajos	Comida

camisa	azul	azafata	fontanero
carne	rosado	abogado	pollo
traje	cocinero	queso	corbata
naranja	sombrero	arroz	rojo

6. (Free time) Complete with *hago*, *voy* or *juego* as appropriate

a. No _____ deporte

b. Nunca _____ al baloncesto

c. _____ al gimnasio a menudo

d. _____ pesas todos los días

e. Siempre _____ a la Play

f. No _____ a la piscina hoy

7. Complete with the missing verb, choosing from the list below

a. _____ mucho zumo de fruta

b. Me _____ las fresas

c. Después de hacer mis deberes _____ al gimnasio o _____ a los videojuegos

d. _____ mucho deporte

e. Por la mañana no _____ mucho. Solo dos tostadas

f. Mi padre _____ como ingeniero. Yo no _____ todavía. _____ estudiante

g. No me _____ ver dibujos animados. _____ ver series en Netflix

h. Por la mañana, me _____ a eso de las seis

levanto	juego	encantan	trabajo
voy	hago	prefiero	soy
trabaja	bebo	gusta	desayuno

8. Time markers – Translate

a. Nunca:

b. De vez en cuando:

c. Siempre:

d. Todos los días:

e. Raramente:

f. Una vez por semana:

g. Dos veces al mes:

9. Split sentences (Relationships)

Me llevo bien con	mis abuelos
No me llevo	mi madre
Mis padres	pesado
Me encanta	bien con mi madre
Mi hermano es	de arte es estricto
Mi profesor	son generosos
Mi novia es muy	porque es malo
Odio a mi tío	amable
No soporto	gusta muchísimo
Mi novio me	a mi hermana

11. Translate into Spanish

a. I play tennis every day

b. I wear a jacket sometimes

c. I go to the gym often

d. I don't watch cartoons

e. I get up at around 6 a.m.

f. I shower twice a day

10. Complete the translation

a. Mi hermano es _____

 My brother is a fireman

b. No _____. Soy _____

I don't work. I am a student

c. De vez en cuando _____ al cine con mi padre

From time to time I go to the cinema with my father

d. Nunca _____ la tele *I never watch tv*

e. No _____ a mis profesores

I don't hate my teachers

f. Mis padres son _____

My parents are strict

g. Nunca _____ _____ *I never go jogging*

UNIT 17
Describing my house:
- indicating where it is located
- saying what I like/dislike about it

In this unit you will learn how to say in Spanish

- Where your house/apartment is located
- What your favourite room is
- What you like to do in each room
- The present indicative of key reflexive verbs in -AR

You will revisit:
- Adjectives to describe places
- Frequency markers
- Countries

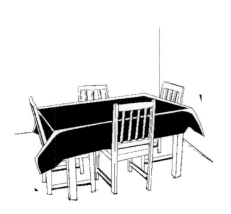

UNIT 17
Describing my house

Vivo en una casa *I live in a ... house*	**bonita** *beautiful* **fea** *ugly* **grande** *big* **nueva** *new* **pequeña** *small* **vieja** *old*	**en las afueras** *on the outskirts* **en el campo** *in the countryside* **en el centro de la ciudad** *in the city centre*	**En mi casa hay cuatro/cinco/seis habitaciones** *in my house there are 4/5/6 rooms* **Mi habitación favorita es...** *my favourite room is*	**la cocina** *the kitchen* **el comedor** *the dining room* **el cuarto de baño** *the bathroom* **mi dormitorio** *my bedroom*
Vivo en un piso *I live in a ... flat*	**bonito** *beautiful* **feo** *ugly* **grande** *big* **nuevo** *new* **pequeño** *small* **viejo** *old*	**en la costa** *on the coast* **en la montaña** *in the mountain* **en una zona residencial** *in a residential area*	**Me gusta relajarme en...** *I like to relax in* **Me gusta trabajar en...** *I like to work in* **Siempre me ducho en...** *I always shower in*	**el jardín** *the garden* **el salón** *the living room* **la terraza** *the terrace*

Unit 17. Describing my house: VOCABULARY BUILDING PART 1

1. Match up

vivo en	a flat
una casa	new
un piso	residential
grande	area
nuevo	I live in
el campo	a house
zona	big
residencial	the countryside

2. Translate into English

a. Vivo en una casa pequeña y vieja

b. Vivo en un piso grande y nuevo

c. Mi piso está *(is)* en las afueras

d. Mi casa está en el campo

e. Mi habitación favorita es mi dormitorio

f. Me gusta la cocina

g. Me gusta trabajar en el salón

h. Siempre me ducho en el cuarto de baño

i. Me gusta relajarme en el jardín

3. Complete with the missing words

a. Vivo _____ la costa *I live on the coast*

b. Me _____ mi casa *I like my house*

c. _____ en una casa vieja pero _____

I live in an old but pretty house

d. Me gusta _____ en el salón

I like to relax in the living room

e. Mi _____ está en las _____

My house is on the outskirts

f. ¡Nunca me _____ en el jardín!

I never shower in the garden!

4. Complete the words (about 'una casa')

a. una c_____	*a house*	g. la c_____	*the coast*
b. f_____	*ugly*	h. las a_____	*the outskirts*
c. n_____	*new*	i. el c_____	*the centre*
d. v_____	*old*	j. el j_____	*the garden*
e. g_____	*big*	k. la t_____	*the terrace*
f. e_____	*in*	l. mi d_____	*my room*

5. Classify the words/phrases below in the table below

a. **siempre**
b. relajarme
c. nunca
d. bonito
e. nuevo
f. montaña
g. me ducho
h. dormitorio
i. grande
j. a veces
k. comedor
l. campo
m. pequeño
n. trabajar
o. costa
p. vivo

Time phrases	Nouns	Verbs	Adjectives
a.			

6. Translate into Spanish

a. I live in an old flat

b. I live in a new house

c. In the town centre

d. I like to relax in the living room

e. I always shower in the bathroom

f. I live in a residential area

g. My favourite room is the kitchen

Unit 17. Describing my house: VOCABULARY BUILDING PART 2

1. Match up

vivo en	costa
una casa	residencial
en la	un piso
un piso	bonita
en el	moderno
una zona	relajarme
siempre me	centro
me gusta	ducho

2. Complete with the missing word

a. No me gusta _____   *I don't like to work*

b. Es pequeño pero _____   *It is small but pretty*

c. Está en el _____ de la ciudad   *It is in the town centre*

d. Está en las _____   *It is on the outskirts*

e. Vivo en una _____ grande   *I live in a big house*

f. En una _____ residencial   *In a residential area*

g. Mi _____ favorita es...   *My favourite room is...*

h. Me relajo en el _____   *I relax in the garden*

i. Estudio en mi _____   *I study in my bedroom*

j. _____ cuatro habitaciones   *There are four rooms*

zona	trabajar	afueras	centro	jardín
casa	dormitorio	bonito	habitación	hay

3. Translate into English

a. Vivo en una casa pequeña

b. Está en la costa

c. Un piso grande pero feo

d. Está en una zona residencial

e. En mi casa hay cinco habitaciones

f. Me gusta trabajar en el comedor

g. Me gusta relajarme

h. Vivo en una casa en la costa

i. Vivo en las afueras de la ciudad

4. Broken words

a. Me gusta re_____   *I like to relax*

b. Vivo en la m_____   *I live in the mountain*

c. El centro de la ci_____   *The city centre*

d. Nunca me d_____...   *I never shower...*

e. ...en el j_____   *...in the garden*

f. Mi habitación f_____ es...   *My favourite room is...*

g. Mi do_____   *My bedroom*

5. 'El, 'La' or 'Las'?

a. _____**La**_____costa

b. _____ campo

c. _____ comedor

d. _____ salón

e. _____ ciudad

f. _____ jardín

g. _____ cuarto de baño

h. _____ habitación

i. _____ afueras

j. _____ zona

6. Bad translation: spot any fix the translation errors

a. Vivo en una casa en la costa *I live in a flat on the coast*

b. Mi habitación favorita es la cocina
My favourite room is the dining room

c. Me gusta relajarme en mi dormitorio
I like to work out in my bedroom

d. Vivo en un piso en una zona residencial
I live in a house in a residential area

e. Me gusta mi casa porque es grande y bonita
I don't like my house because it is big and ugly

f. Me gusta trabajar en el salón *I like to work in a saloon*

g. En mi casa hay cuatro habitaciones
In my house there are fourteen rooms

Unit 17. Describing my house: READING

Me llamo Dante. Soy de Italia. Vivo en una casa grande y bonita en la costa. Me gusta mucho. En mi casa hay diez habitaciones y mi habitación favorita es la cocina. Me gusta cocinar *(to cook)* en la cocina con mi madre. Siempre me levanto, me ducho en el cuarto de baño y luego me visto en mi dormitorio.

Mi amigo Pablo vive en una casa pequeña en la montaña. Pablo es muy gracioso y trabajador. No le gusta su casa porque es muy pequeña.

Me llamo Miquel y soy de Barcelona, en Cataluña. Mi casa está en el centro de la ciudad, y vivo cerca de la costa. En mi casa hablo catalán y español; el catalán es una lengua muy antigua y bonita. Vivo en una casa pequeña, nueva y muy bonita. Hay seis habitaciones y también tengo un jardín grande. Mi caballo vive en el jardín. Se llama Paco (el caballo, no el jardín). Mi habitación favorita en mi casa es el comedor porque me gusta mucho comer.

Me gusta relajarme en mi dormitorio. Siempre veo dibujos animados y series en Netflix. También me gusta trabajar aquí, cuando tengo deberes por ejemplo.

Me llamo Lenny. Soy italiano y vivo en una casa muy vieja pero muy bonita en el campo, en Italia. ¡Me encanta mi casa! En mi casa hay 5 habitaciones pero mi habitación favorita es el salón. Todos los días, después del colegio me gusta relajarme en el salón y ver la televisión con mi hermana. ¡No me gusta el cuarto de baño porque a veces hay ratas!

Me llamo Ariella. Soy de Cuba. Siempre me despierto a las cinco de la mañana porque vivo lejos del colegio, en las afueras de la ciudad. Vivo en un piso en un edificio muy viejo. El piso es muy viejo y un poco feo, pero me gusta. Me gusta relajarme en mi dormitorio. A veces leo libros y a veces escucho música en Spotify. Mi dormitorio es mi habitación favorita.

1. Answer the following questions about Dante

a. Where is he from?

b. What is his house like?

c. How many rooms are there in his house?

d. Which is his favourite room?

e. Where does he get dressed?

f. Where does Pablo live?

g. Does he like his house? (Why?)

2. Find the Spanish for the phrases below in Miquel's text

a. my house is in the centre

b. I live near…

c. I speak Catalan and Spanish

d. I also have a garden

e. I really like to eat

f. he lives in the garden

g. I like to relax

h. I like to work here

4. Find the Spanish for the following phrases/sentences in Ariella's text

a. I am from Cuba

b. I always wake up at 5

c. I live far from school

d. The flat is very old

e. …and a bit ugly

f. But I like it

g. Sometimes I read books

3. Find Someone Who…

a. …lives far from school

b. …speaks two languages

c. …has a really really big house

d. …sometimes finds 'unwanted guests' in the bathroom

e. …has a big pet that lives outside the house

f. …listens to music on a streaming platform

g. …is a foodie (loves food)

h. …has a friend that doesn't like their own house

Unit 17. Describing my house: TRANSLATION

1. Gapped translation

a. **Vivo en las afueras** *I live on the* _____

b. **Mi casa es muy grande pero un poco fea**

My house is _____ *big but* ___ _____ *ugly*

c. **Está en la montaña** *It is in the* _____

d. **Vivo en el centro** _____ _____ _____

I live in the city centre

e. **En mi casa** _____ **cinco habitaciones**

In my house there are five rooms

f. **No me gusta mucho la** _____ **porque es** _____

I don't really like the kitchen because it's ugly

2. Translate to English

a. la costa

b. un piso

c. vivo en

d. el centro

e. de la ciudad

f. mi habitacón favorita

g. me gusta relajarme

h. mi dormitorio

i. el salón

3. Translate into English

a. Vivo en un piso pequeño y feo

b. Mi casa es moderna pero bastante bonita

c. Mi piso es viejo pero me gusta mucho

d. Vivo en una casa en la costa

e. En mi casa hay cinco habitaciones

f. Mi habitación favorita es mi dormitorio

4. Translate into Spanish

a. Big: G_____

b. Small: P_____

c. Outskirts: A_____

d. Coast: C_____

e. Area: Z_____

f. Residential: R_____

g. Ugly: F_____

h. Room: H_____

i. There are: H_____

j. Old: V_____

5. Translate into Spanish

a. I live in a small house

b. In the city centre

c. In my house there are...

d. Seven rooms

e. My favourite room is...

f. The living room

g. I like to relax in my bedroom

h. And I like to work in the living room

i. I live in a small and old flat

j. In a residential area

 **THE LANGUAGE GYM**

Grammar Time 14: VIVIR – to live

(yo) vivo *I live* **(tú) vives** *you* **(él) vive** *he* **(ella) vive** *she* **(nosotros) vivimos** *we* **(vosotros) vivís** *you guys* **(vosotras) vivís** *you ladies* **(ellos) viven** *they -masculine/mixed-* **(ellas) viven** *they -female-*	**en una casa**	**acogedora** *cosy* **bonita** *beautiful* **espaciosa** *spacious* **fea** *ugly* **grande** *big* **nueva** *new* **pequeña** *small* **vieja** *old*	**en las afueras** *on the outskirts* **en el campo** *in the countryside* **en el centro de la ciudad** *in the city centre*
	en un piso	**acogedor** *cosy* **bonito** *beautiful* **espacioso** *spacious* **feo** *ugly* **grande** *big* **nuevo** *new* **pequeño** *small* **viejo** *old*	**en la costa** *on the coast* **en la montaña** *in the mountain* **en una zona residencial** *in a residential area*

1. Match

viven	I live
vivimos	you live
vive	he/she lives
vivo	we live
vivís	you guys live
vives	they live

3. Complete with the correct form of 'vivir'

a. Mi madre y yo _____ en

Barcelona. Mi padre _____ en Madrid.

b. (vosotros) ¿Dónde _____?

c. Yo _____ en Londres. Mi hermano

_____ en Roma.

d. Mis tíos _____ en Estados Unidos.

f. Mi novia no _____ aquí.

g. (yo) _____ en una casa muy grande

en las afueras

h. (tú) ¡_____ en una casa enorme!

5. Complete the translation

a. My siblings live in the countryside

Mis _____ _____ en el _____

b. I live in a flat _____ *en un* _____

c. My mother doesn't live with my father

Mi madre no _____ _____ mi padre

d. We live on the outskirts

_____ *en las* _____

e. Where do you live? ¿Dónde _____?

f. They live in a small house

(Ellos) _____ *en una* _____ _____.

2. Complete with the correct form of 'vivir'

a. _____ en una casa bonita

I live in a beautiful house

b. ¿Dónde _____ tú? *Where do you live?*

c. _____ en Londres desde hace tres años

We have been living in London for three years

d. _____ en una casa en la costa

He/she lives in a house on the coast

e. ¿ _____ en una casa o en un piso?

Do you live in a house or in a flat?

f. _____ en un piso antiguo

They live in an old flat

g. _____ en las afueras

We live on the outskirts

h. Mi padre _____ en una granja

My father lives on a farm

4. Spot and correct the errors

a. (yo) No vives en el centro de la ciudad

b. Mis padres vivimos aquí

c. Mi novia viven en un piso en la costa

d. Mi madre y yo vivís en las afueras

e. Mis hermanos no vive con nosotros

f. Mi abuelo materno vivo con nosostros

6. Translate into Spanish

a. My parents and I live in a cosy house

b. My mother lives in a small house on the coast

c. My cousins live in a beautiful house in the countryside

d. My girlfriend lives in a modern flat in the centre

e. My sisters live in an old flat on the ouskirts

f. My best friend Paco lives in a spacious flat near the town centre

 THE LANGUAGE GYM

Grammar Time 15: Reflexives (Part 1)

USEFUL VOCABULARY

Afeitarse	To shave
Bañarse	To bathe
Cepillarse	To brush one's teeth
Ducharse	To shower
Llamarse	To be called
Lavarse	To wash
Levantarse	To get up
Relajarse	To rest
Peinarse	To comb one's hair
Prepararse	To get ready

Present Indicative of AR verbs ending in SE

	Lavarse	**Ducharse**
(yo)	me lavo	me ducho
(tú)	te lavas	te duchas
(él) (ella)	se lava	se ducha
(nosotros)	nos lavamos	nos duchamos
(vosotros)	os laváis	os ducháis
(ellos) (ellas)	se lavan	se duchan

1. Complete with me, se or nos

a. (ellos) _____ levantan

b. (yo) _____ ducho

c. (ella) _____ queja

d. (nosotros) _____ lavamos

e. (él) _____ cepilla los dientes

f. (nosotros) _____ peinamos

g. (ellas) _____ relajan

h. (ellas) _____ arreglan

2. Complete with the correct form of the verb

a. (ella – cepillarse) ____ _____ los dientes

b. (nosotros – ducharse) _____ _____ enseguida

c. (él – cansarse) ____ _____ mucho durante las clases de educación física

d. (él - afeitarse) nunca ____ _____ _____

e. (ella – relajarse) nunca ____ _____ _____

f. (ellos – levantarse) ____ _____ temprano

g. (él – quejarse) siempre ____ _____

3. Translate into English

a. Me levanto a eso de las seis, pero mi hermano se levanta a eso de las siete. Yo me ducho enseguida pero mi hermano nunca se ducha.

b. Mi hermana se relaja antes de ir al colegio. Ella siempre se mira en el espejo.

c. Me afeito casi todos los días. Mi padre se afeita todos los días.

d. Mis padres se levantan más temprano que yo. Luego se lavan y toman el desayuno antes de nosotros.

e. Mi padre es calvo, por lo tanto, nunca se peina.

f. Mi madre tiene muchísimo pelo. Ella se peina por media hora antes de salir de casa.

g. No tenemos una bañera en mi casa. Por lo tanto, nos duchamos pero no nos bañamos.

h. Yo me cepillo los dientes cinco veces al día. En cambio, mi hermano se cepilla los dientes solo una vez al día.

 **THE LANGUAGE GYM**

Yo me levanto después de mi padre, media hora más tarde, a eso de las seis y media. Me lavo, me ducho, me afeito, me peino y finalmente me visto y voy a la cocina. Desayuno solo. Como cereales con leche, unas tostadas con mermelada y bebo un café con leche. Luego, me cepillo los dientes, me arreglo para ir al colegio y a eso de las siete salgo de casa. (Mario, 14)

5. Find the Spanish in Mario's text

a. I get up

b. I wash

c. I comb my hair

d. I brush my teeth

e. I get ready

f. I shave

g. I shower

h. I drink

i. I leave the house

6. Complete

a. Me duch__   *I shower*

b. Se afeit__   *He shaves*

c. Nos duch__ __ __ __   *We shower*

d. Os lav__ __ __   *You guys wash*

e. Me prepar__   *I prepare myself*

f. Se pein__ __   *They comb their hair*

g. Me cepill__ los dientes   *I brush my teeth*

h. Se bañ__ __   *They bathe*

8. Translate

a. Normally, I shower at seven o'clock

b. He never brushes his teeth

c. We shave three times a week

d. They get up early

e. He never combs his hair

f. I don't bathe

g. We prepare ourselves for school

h. They never relax

4. Find in Felipe's text (below) the Spanish for:

a. They get up

b. My father gets up

c. He showers

d. He gets ready

e. My mother gets up

f. He leaves the house

g. He shaves

h. He combs his hair

Mis padres se levantan muy temprano. Mi madre se levanta a eso de las cinco y media, para preparar el desayuno para mi padre y para nosotros. Antes de preparar el desayuno, se ducha, se viste, se arregla y toma un café viendo la tele. Mi padre se levanta media hora más tarde. Se ducha, se afeita, se peina, se viste y luego toma el desayuno con mi madre en la cocina. Él sale de casa media hora más tarde, a eso de las seis y media. (Felipe, 12)

7. Complete

a. _____ _____ a las seis

They get up at six

b. _____ _____ a las siete

They shave at seven

c. _____ _____ temprano

I get up early

d. Nunca _____ _____

He never shaves

e. _____ _____ los dientes después de comer

We brush our teeth after eating

f. Siempre _____ _____ en el espejo

She always looks at herself in the mirror

UNIT 18
Saying what I do at home, how often, when and where

In this unit you will learn how to provide a more detailed account of your daily activities building on the vocabulary learnt in the previous unit.

You will revisit:
- Time markers
- Reflexive verbs
- Parts of the house
- Description of people and places
- Telling the time
- Nationalities
- The verbs 'hacer', 'jugar' and 'ir'

Unit 18
Saying what I do at home, how often, when and where

A eso de las seis, de la mañana *At around 6 a.m.*	**charlo con mi madre** *I chat with my mum*	**en la cocina** *in the kitchen*
	desayuno *I have breakfast*	
	descanso *I rest*	**en el comedor** *in the dining room*
A menudo *Often*	**escucho música** *I listen to music*	
	hago mis deberes *I do my homework*	**en el cuarto de baño** *in the bathroom*
A veces *Sometimes*	**juego a la Play** *I play Playstation*	
	leo revistas *I read magazines*	**en el dormitorio de mi hermano** *in my brother's bedroom*
Cuando tengo tiempo *When I have time*	**leo tebeos** *I read comics*	**en el dormitorio de mis padres** *in my parents' bedroom*
	me lavo los dientes *I brush my teeth*	
Dos veces a la semana *Twice a week*	**me meto en Internet** *I go on the Internet*	**en mi dormitorio** *in my bedroom*
	me visto *I get dressed*	
		en el garaje *in the garage*
Nunca *Never*	**monto en bici** *I ride my bike*	
	preparo la comida *I prepare food*	**en el jardín** *in the garden*
Por lo general *Usually*	**salgo de casa** *I leave the house*	
	subo fotos a Instagram *I upload pics to Instagram*	**en la sala de juegos** *in the games room*
Siempre *Always*	**veo la tele** *I watch television*	**en el salón** *in the living room*
	veo películas *I watch films*	**en la terraza** *in the terrace*
Todos los días *Every day*	**veo series en Netflix** *I watch series on Netflix*	

Unit 18. Saying what I do at home: VOCABULARY BUILDING PART 1

1. Match up

Leo tebeos	I chat with
Veo películas	I wash
Preparo la comida	I watch movies
Leo revistas	I prepare food
Me visto	I read magazines
Charlo con	I shower
Me lavo	I get dressed
Me ducho	I read comics

2. Complete with the missing words

a. Me _____ *I get dressed*

b. Leo _____ *I read comics*

c. Leo _____ *I read magazines*

d. Me lavo los _____ *I wash my teeth*

e. Me _____ *I shower*

f. _____ la comida *I prepare food*

g. Me _____ en Internet *I go on the Net*

h. Escucho _____ *I listen to music*

i. _____ fotos a Instagram
I upload photos onto Instagram

3. Translate into English

a. Por lo general me ducho a eso de las siete de la mañana

b. Nunca preparo la comida

c. Por lo general leo revistas en el salón

d. A eso de las siete de la mañana desayuno en el comedor

e. De vez en cuando charlo con mi madre en la cocina

f. A veces desayuno en la cocina

g. A veces juego a la Play con mi hermano en la sala de juegos

h. Siempre salgo de casa a las ocho de la mañana

4. Complete the words

a. Me d_____ *I shower* g. Me v_____*I get dressed*

b. L_____*I read* h. J_____*I play*

c. C_____*I chat* i. S_____*I leave*

d. P_____*I prepare* j. H_____*I do*

e. S_____*I upload* k. M_____*I ride*

f. Me l_____*I wash* l. V_____*I watch*

5. Classify the words/phrases below in the table below

a. **a eso de las seis**   i. me lavo los dientes
b. siempre   j. a veces
c. nunca   k. todos los días
d. mi dormitorio   l. escucho música
e. veo la tele   m. leo tebeos
f. juego a la Play   n. monto en bici
g. me lavo   o. dos veces a la semana
h. subo fotos a Instagram   p. chateo por Skype

Time phrases	Rooms in the house	Things you do in the bathroom	Free-time activities
a.			

6. Fill in the table with what activities you do in which room

Juego a la Play	En mi dormitorio
Veo la tele	
Me ducho	
Hago mis deberes	
Me lavo los dientes	
Descanso	
Preparo la comida	

Unit 18. Saying what I do at home: VOCABULARY BUILDING PART 2

7. Complete the table

English	Español
I get dressed	
I shower	
	Hago mis deberes
I upload photos	
	Salgo de casa
	Charlo con mi hermano
I rest	

8. Multiple choice quiz

	A	B	C
Nunca	always	never	sometimes
A veces	sometimes	always	never
Dormitorio	bedroom	lounge	garden
Me lavo	I shave	I wash	I go out
Me ducho	I shower	I go out	I rest
Descanso	I go out	I watch	I rest
Jardín	garden	garage	kitchen
Cocina	bedroom	lounge	kitchen
Juego	I rest	I play	I prepare
Leo	I watch	I read	I play
Salgo	I go out	I rest	I read
Siempre	always	never	every day

9. Anagrams: unscramble & translate

(Example) Ncanu - *nunca* - *never*

a. cinoCa

b. goSal

c. oeL

d. emSipre

e. uboS tofos

f. oval eM

10. Broken words

a. La co_____ *Kitchen*

b. Nun_____ *Never*

c. A vec_____ *Sometimes*

d. Sie_____ *Always*

e. A men_____ *Often*

f. Los te_____ *Comics*

g. Mi dor_____ *My bedroom*

h. Sa_____ *I go out*

i. Ch_____ *I chat*

11. Complete based on the translation in brackets

a. A e_____ d____ l___ s_____ y media, m__ l_____ l____ d_____ *At around seven thirty, I brush my teeth*

b. A e_____ d_____ l____ o_____ y cuarto, d_____ *At around a quarter past eight I have breakfast*

c. A v_____ p_____ l___ c_____ *Sometimes I prepare the food*

d. S_____ v_____ l___ t_____ mientras d_____ *I always watch TV when I have breakfast*

e. P___ l___ g_____, s_____ d___ c_____ a l____ o_____ y media *Generally, I leave the house at eight thirty*

f. L____ t_____ r_____ *I read comics rarely*

g. A e_____ d___ l_____ c_____ h_____ m_____ d_____ *At around five I do my homework*

12. Gap-fill from memory

a. A veces _____ tebeos

b. Siempre me _____ los dientes después de comer

c. _____ series en Netflix todos los días

d. Nunca _____ revistas de moda

e. Nunca _____ mis deberes

f. _____ fotos a Instagram a menudo

g. En el fin de semana _____ en bici

h. _____ de casa a eso de las ocho

i. _____ música a menudo

THE LANGUAGE GYM

Unit 18. Saying what I do at home: READING

Me llamo Fabián. Soy de Gibraltar. Tengo un perro en casa. Siempre me levanto temprano, a las cinco y cuarto. Luego, voy al gimnasio y hago deporte. Me ducho cuando vuelvo a casa. Pero mi hermano Joe es muy perezoso e inactivo. Se levanta a las siete. Joe nunca juega al fútbol, y nunca hace deporte. Por eso está muy muy gordo. Por la tarde, leo tebeos en mi dormitorio o escucho música. Entre semana cuando vuelvo a casa hago mis deberes en el salón con mi madre. Me gusta porque ella es muy inteligente y siempre me ayuda. Finalmente, me acuesto a las nueve, en mi dormitorio, claro.

Me llamo Valentino. Soy italiano. Siempre me despierto temprano, a eso de las seis y media. Luego me ducho y me lavo los dientes en el cuarto de baño. No desayuno nada por la mañana pero mi hermana Valeria desayuna cereales en el comedor con mi padre. Voy al colegio a pie. Vuelvo a casa a eso de las tres y media y luego me relajo un poco. Por lo general veo la tele en el salón. Luego navego por internet, veo una serie en Netflix o veo videos de TikTok en mi habitación. Luego, a las ocho, preparo la comida con mi madre en la cocina. Me encanta preparar ensaladas porque son deliciosas. Me acuesto tarde, a las diez.

Me llamo Eduardo y vivo en Dinamarca. Todos los días me levanto a las cinco de la mañana. Luego me ducho y tomo el desayuno en el jardín. Salgo de casa a las siete y voy al colegio a caballo. Cuando vuelvo a casa chateo por Skype con mi familia en Inglaterra y me meto en internet, en mi dormitorio. Luego monto en bici en el jardín con mis dos perros. A veces veo dibujos animados y subo fotos a Instagram en el dormitorio de mi hermano. Mi hermano Samuel sube videos a TikTok de sus bailes nuevos. Me gusta mucho mi hermano porque es muy divertido y activo. ¡Baila muy bien! Siempre charlo y juego a las cartas con él. Samuel es mi mejor amigo en el mundo.

1. Answer the following questions about Fabián

a. Where is he from?

b. What animal does he have?

c. What does he do after he wakes up?

d. Why is Joe fat?

e. Where does he do his homework on weekdays?

f. Who helps him with his homework?

g. Where does he go to bed?

2. Find the Spanish for the phrases below in Eduardo's text

a. I get up

b. then I shower

c. I go to school

d. by horse

e. I go on the internet

f. uploads videos to TikTok

g. new dances

h. I always chat

3. Find Someone Who

a. ...wakes up earliest

b. ...gets helps with their homework from a family member

c. ...likes to watch videos of people dancing

d. ...has nothing for breakfast

e. ...has a really lazy brother

f. ...likes to prepare healthy food

g. ...has a family member that is their best friend

h. ...goes to school in the most exciting way

4. Find the Spanish for the following phrases/ in Valentino's text

a. I am Italian

b. I wake up early

c. I have nothing for breakfast

d. Valeria eats cereals

e. In the dining room

f. In the living room

g. I watch TikTok videos

Unit 18. Saying what I do at home: WRITING

1. Split sentences

Charlo	comida
Descanso en	temprano
Preparo la	con mi madre
Subo fotos	mi dormitorio
Hago mis	los dientes
Me levanto muy	a Instagram
Juego con mi	ordenador
Me lavo	deberes

2. Complete with the correct option

a. Me levanto a las seis de la _____

b. Juego al fútbol en el _____

c. Veo la tele en el _____

d. Escucho música en mi _____

e. Preparo la _____ con mi padre

f. Me _____ los dientes

g. _____ dibujos animados

h. _____ al colegio a caballo

salón	mañana	lavo	dormitorio
voy	comida	veo	jardín

3. Spot and correct the grammar and spelling mistakes note: in some cases a word is missing

a. me ducha en el cuarto de bano

b. desayuno en el coccina

c. en mi dormitoria

d. juego con la ordenator

e. salga casa a ocho

f. hago mi deberes

g. veo serias en Netflix

h. voy a la colegio a cabballo

i. el dormitorio mi hermano

4. Complete the words

a. des_____ *I have breakfast*

b. la co_____ *the kitchen*

c. mi d_____ *my bedroom*

d. el g_____ *the garage*

e. s_____ de c_____ *I leave the house*

f. en el s_____ *in the living room*

g. en el c_____ *in the dining room*

h. en el c_____ d____ b_____
in the bathroom

i. v_____p_____ e__ e___
d_____ d__ m__ h_____
I watch films in my brother's bedroom

5. Guided writing – write 3 short paragraphs in the first person I using the details below

Person	Gets up	Showers	Has breakfast	Goes to school	Evening activity 1	Evening activity 2
Gonzalo	6.15	In bathroom	Kitchen	With brother	Watch tv in living room	Prepare food in the kitchen
Mauricio	7.30	In shower	Dining room	With mother	Read book in bedroom	Talk to family on skype
Isidora	6.45	In bathroom	Living room	With Uncle	Listen to music in garden	Upload photos to instagram

Grammar Time 16: JUGAR, (Part 3) HACER (Part 3) IR (Part 2)

1. Complete with 'Hago', 'Juego' or 'Voy'

a. _____ mis deberes

b. _____ al ajedrez

c. _____ a España

d. _____ a la piscina

e. _____ en el ordenador

f. _____ natación

g. _____ al tenis

h. No _____ nada

3. Complete with the appropriate verb

a. Mi madre _____ a la iglesia todos los sábados

b. Mi hermana nunca _____ sus deberes

c. (nosotros) _____ al baloncesto todos los días

d. Mis padres no _____ mucho deporte

e. Mis hermanos _____ al ajedrez a menudo

f. Mi novia y yo _____ al colegio a pie

g. ¿Qué _____ tú?

h. (vosotros) ¿Adónde _____?

i. ¿Qué trabajo _____ tú?

j. Mi primo _____ al fútbol con nosotros

k. Mis tíos _____ al estadio a menudo

l. Mi padre _____ al tenis de vez en cuando

m. En el verano, mis padres y yo _____ vela

n. En el fin de semana mis padres no _____ nada

2. Complete with the missing forms of the present indicative of the verbs below

	Hacer	Ir	Jugar
yo *I*		voy	juego
tú *you*	haces		
él, ella *he/she*			
nosotros nosotras *we*			
vosotros vosotras *you guys/ladies*	hacéis		jugáis
ellos, ellas *they*		van	

4. Complete with the 'nosotros' form of jugar/hacer/ir

a. _____ al rugby

b. _____ a la iglesia

c. _____ al baloncesto

d. _____ al colegio

e. _____ al tenis

f. _____ al parque

g. _____ al cricket

h. _____ a la piscina

i. _____ deporte

j. _____ vela

k. _____ footing

l. _____ al ajedrez

5. Complete with the 'ellos' form of the verbs

a. _____ a las damas

b. _____ al estadio

c. _____ escalada

d. _____ sus deberes

e. _____ surf

f. _____ a la playa

g. _____ a casa

h. _____ al voleibol

i. _____ al tenis

j. _____ footing

k. _____ pesas

l. _____ al cricket

Present Indicative of -AR reflexive verbs

	Lavarse	Ducharse
yo	me lavo	me ducho
tú	te lavas	te duchas
él ella	se lava	se ducha
nosotros	nos lavamos	nos duchamos
vosotros	os laváis	os ducháis
ellos ellas	se lavan	se duchan

USEFUL VOCABULARY

Afeitarse	To shave
Bañarse	To bathe
Cepillarse	To brush one's teeth
Ducharse	To shower
Llamarse	To be called
Lavarse	To wash
Levantarse	To get up
Relajarse	To relax
Peinarse	To comb one's hair
Prepararse	To get ready

6. Translate into Spanish

a. We play on the computer often

b. My brother never does weight lifting

c. My sister plays netball every day

d. My father never does sport

e. What job do you guys do?

f. Where do you go after school?

g. My brother and I often play chess

h. My parents and I go swimming once a week

i. My brother never goes to church

j. My best friend goes to the stadium every Saturday

7. Complete with the correct ending

a. Mi madre se llam____ Marina

b. Mi hermano no se lav____

c. (yo) Me duch____ a menudo

d. Mi padre se afeit____ todos los días

e. Primero, me ducho, luego me pein____

f. Nos levant_____ a eso de las siete

g. ¿Cuándo te duch____?

h. ¿Mi hermano nunca se lav____?

i. ¿Cómo os llam____?

8. Translate into Spanish

a. We get up at six

b. He showers, then shaves

c. I shower at around seven

d. My father never shaves

e. My brothers never wash

f. He is called Miguel

g. They have a bath

h. She gets up late

i. He doesn't brush his teeth

j. When do you rest?

 THE LANGUAGE GYM

UNIT 19
My holiday plans
(Talking about future plans for holidays)

In this unit you will learn how to talk about:

- What you intend to do in future holidays
- Where you are going to go
- Where you are going to stay
- Who you are going to travel with
- How it will be
- Means of transport

You will revisit:
- The verb 'ir'
- Free-time activities
- Previously seen adjectives

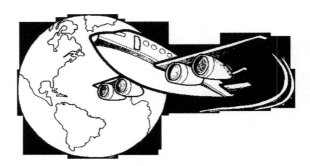

UNIT 19
My holiday plans

Este verano *This summer* **Voy a ir de vacaciones a** *I am going to go on holiday to* **Vamos a ir de vacaciones a** *We are going to go on holiday to*	Argentina Chile Cuba España México	**en autocar** *by coach* **en avión** *by plane* **en barco** *by boat* **en coche** *by car*	
Voy a pasar... *I am going to spend* **Vamos a pasar...** *We are going to spend*	**una semana** *1 week* **dos semanas** *2 weeks*	**allí** *there* **con mi familia** *with my family*	**Será aburrido** *it will be boring*
Voy a quedarme en *I am going to stay in* **Vamos a quedarnos en** *We are going to stay in*	**la casa de mi familia** **un camping** **un hotel barato** *a cheap hotel* **un hotel de lujo** *a luxury hotel*		**Será divertido** *it will be fun*
Voy a... *I am going to...* **Vamos a** *We are going to...* **Me gustaría...** *I would like to...* **Nos gustaría...** *We would like to...*	**bailar** *dance* **comer y dormir** *eat and sleep* **comer comida deliciosa** *eat delicious food* **comprar recuerdos** *buy souvenirs* **descansar** *rest* **hacer buceo** *go diving* **hacer deporte** *do sport* **hacer turismo** *go sightseeing* **ir a la playa** *go to the beach* **ir de compras** *go shopping* **ir de marcha** *go clubbing* **jugar con mis amigos** *play with my friends* **montar en bici** *go biking* **salir al centro** *go out into town* **tocar el ukelele** *play the ukulele* **tomar el sol** *sunbathe*		**Será guay** *it will be cool*

Unit 19. My holiday plans: VOCABULARY BUILDING

1. Match up

voy a ir	I'm going to spend
voy a pasar	a campsite
voy a quedarme	I'm going to go
un hotel barato	it will be cool
un camping	I'm going to stay
me gustaría	to buy
comprar	a cheap hotel
será guay	I would like to

2. Complete with the missing word

a. Comer y _____ *To eat and sleep*

b. Voy a _____ *I am going to rest*

c. Me _____ ir a… *I would like to go to…*

d. _____ con mis amigos *To play with my friends*

e. _____ ___ quedarme en… *I am going to stay in…*

f. _____ aburrido *It will be boring*

g. Vamos a _____ *We are going to spend…*

h. Voy a viajar en _____ *I'm going to travel by plane*

i. Voy a pasar dos semanas _____ con mi _____
I am going to spend two weeks there with my family

3. Translate into English

a. Este verano voy a ir a Grecia

b. Voy a pasar tres semanas allí

c. Voy a ir a Cuba en avión

d. Vamos a ir de compras

e. Me gustaría salir al centro

f. Voy a jugar con mis amigos

g. Nos gustaría comer y dormir

h. Voy a descansar todos los días

i. Voy a hacer deporte con mi hermano

4. Broken words

a. Com____ y dorm_____ *To eat and sleep*

b. Vamos a qu_____ *We are going to stay*

c. Voy a p_____ *I am going to spend*

d. Me g_____ ir a… *I would like to go to…*

e. Ir a la p_____ *To go to the beach*

f. M_____ en bici *To go biking*

g. T_____ el sol *To sunbathe*

h. S_____ relajante *It will be relaxing*

5. 'Ir', 'Jugar' or 'Hacer'?

a. _____ de compras

b. _____ al centro

c. _____ turismo

d. _____ al fútbol

e. _____ buceo

f. _____ de marcha

g. _____ en bici

h. _____ deporte

i. _____ al ajedrez

j. _____ a la playa

6. Bad translation – spot any translation errors and fix them

a. Este verano vamos a ir a…: *Last summer I am going to go to…*

b. Voy a ir a Argentina con mi padre: *I am going to go to Argentina with my mother*

c. Voy a comer y dormir: *I am going to drink and sleep*

d. Me gustaría descansar mucho: *I would like to rest a bit*

e. Vamos a quedarnos en un hotel: *I am going to stay in a hotel*

f. Voy a pasar una semana allí: *I am going to spend one week here*

g. Vamos a viajar en coche y barco: *I am going to travel by coach and barge*

h. Voy a quedarme en la casa de mi familia: *We are going to stay in my family's house*

Unit 19. My holiday plans: READING (Part 1)

Me llamo Hugo. Soy de Oviedo pero vivo en Madrid. Este verano voy a ir de vacaciones al sur de España, a Cádiz. Voy a viajar en coche con mi novio Alejandro. Vamos a pasar cuatro semanas allí y vamos a ir a la playa todos los días. También vamos a comer comida deliciosa. No voy a hacer turismo porque es muy aburrido. Prefiero tomar el sol en la playa.

Me llamo Deryk y soy de Canadá. En mi familia hay cuatro personas. Mi persona favorita es mi mujer, Anna. Este verano vamos a viajar a Inglaterra y después a Quebec, en Canadá. Voy a descansar y leer libros en Inglaterra y luego voy a hacer esquí y salir con mis amigos en Canadá. Anna va a montar en bici y comer comida deliciosa, como '*poutine*' (similar a patatas fritas con queso). ¡Será guay!

Me llamo Dino. Soy italiano, de Venecia. Este verano voy a ir de vacaciones a México en avión. Voy a pasar dos semanas allí, solo, y voy a quedarme en una caravana en la playa. Voy a visitar monumentos, museos y galerías de arte. No me gusta mucho el deporte, pero me encanta la cultura. Será interesante.

Me llamo Diana. Soy de Polonia pero vivo en China. Este verano voy a viajar a Chile con mi amiga Olivia. Voy a viajar en barco porque tengo mucho tiempo. Voy a pasar cinco semanas allí y voy a quedarme en un hotel de lujo. Me encanta bailar, así que voy a bailar todos los días. También voy a comer y dormir mucho. No voy a ir a museos porque es muy aburrido.

1. Find the Spanish for the following in Hugo's text

a. I am from…

b. But I live in…

c. I am going to travel by…

d. With my boyfriend…

e. We are going to spend…

f. Every day…

g. I am not going to…

h. I prefer to sunbathe…

2. Find the Spanish for the following in Diana's text

a. by boat…

b. I have a lot of time…

c. I am going to spend…

d. I love to dance…

e. so/therefore…

f. also…

g. it is very boring

3. Complete the following statements about Deryk

a. He is from _____

b. His favourite person is _____

c. They will travel to _____ and _____

d. Deryk is going to _____ and _____

e. Anna is going to _____ and _____

f. "Poutine" is made up of _____ and _____

4. List any 8 details about Dino (in 3rd person) in English

1.

2.

3.

4.

5.

6.

7.

8.

5. Find Someone Who...

a. ...likes being out at sea for long periods

b. ...loves learning about culture

c. ...prefers the beach to going sightseeing

d. ...has opposite interests to Dino

e. ...is going to travel by car

 **THE LANGUAGE GYM**

Unit 19. My holiday plans: READING (Part 2)

Me llamo Monserrat. Soy de Barcelona. Tengo una tortuga en casa. Es muy lenta y muy gorda pero me encanta. Es mi mejor amiga. Este verano voy a ir de vacaciones a Málaga, en el sur, con mi familia. Voy a viajar en avión y luego en coche. Vamos a pasar tres semanas en Torremolinos y vamos a quedarnos en un hotel de lujo. ¡Será muy divertido! Luego vamos a ir en coche a Granada y vamos a ver monumentos famosos, como La Alhambra (un palacio árabe muy antiguo). Voy a comer comida deliciosa; me encantan las tapas. También voy a ir de compras todos los días y voy a comprar ropa guay.

Me llamo Freddie. Soy de Buenos Aires, en Argentina. Este verano voy a ir de vacaciones a la ciudad de Cuzco en el sur de Perú, con mi hermano Brian. Vamos a viajar en avión y vamos a pasar dos semanas allí. En Perú vamos a visitar un sitio muy especial: las ruinas Incas de Machu Picchu. Será muy impresionante y divertido. También, en Cuzco vamos a hacer senderismo en la montaña. Será duro pero muy guay. Un día me gustaría descansar y hacer música. Me encanta cantar y a mi hermano Brian le gusta mucho tocar la guitarra. Nuestro grupo favorito se llama Queen. Mi música favorita es la música rock.

Me llamo Josefina y vivo en Granada, en el sur de España. Este verano voy a viajar a Barcelona, en Cataluña, en el noreste de España. Voy a viajar en coche y luego en tren. Voy a pasar dos semanas allí y voy a quedarme en un hotel barato. En Barcelona me gustaría visitar un monumento muy famoso que se llama La Sagrada Familia. Es una catedral muy grande y bonita, diseñada por Antoni Gaudí. También voy a ir a la playa. La playa de Barcelona es un poco fea así que voy a ir en tren a un pueblo que se llama Sitges. ¡La playa allí es espectacular! Tengo una amiga en Sitges que se llama Alicia. Vamos a charlar en la playa y tomar el sol juntas. Será divertido y relajante.

1. Answer the following questions about Montserrat

a. Where is she from?

b. What animal does she have?

c. Who will she go on holiday with?

d. Where will they stay?

e. How will they get to Granada?

f. What is the Alhambra?

g. What will she do every day?

2. Find the Spanish in Josefina's text

a. This summer

b. And then

c. Which is called

d. A cathedral

e. Designed by

f. A bit ugly

g. The beach there

h. Sunbathe together

3. Find Someone Who...

a. ...is going to travel south

b. ...has a brother who is a musician

c. ...has a slow moving pet

d. ...is going to be walking in the mountains

e. ...is going to visit a famous religious monument

f. ...is going to visit a famous palace

g. ...is going to visit the oldest historical site

h. ...is planning to relax on the beach

4. Find the Spanish for the following phrases/sentences in Freddie's text

a. My brother Brian

b. The Incan ruins

c. It will be very impressive

d. It will be tough

e. I would like to rest

f. To play the guitar

g. Our favourite group

h. Rock music

Unit 19. My holiday plans: TRANSLATION/WRITING

1. Gapped translation

a. *I am going to go on holiday:* **Voy a ir de** _____

b. *I am going to travel by car:* **Voy a viajar en** _____

c. *We are going to spend one week there:*

Vamos a _____ **una semana** _____

d. *I am going to stay in a cheap hotel:*

_____ __ **quedarme en un hotel** _____

e. *We are going to eat and sleep every day:*

Vamos __ **comer y** _____ **todos los** _____

f. *When the weather is nice I am going to go to the beach:*
Cuando hace buen _____ **voy a ir a la** _____

g. *I am going to go shopping:* **Voy a ir de** _____

2. Translate to English

a. Comer

b. Comprar

c. Descansar

d. Hacer turismo

e. Ir a la playa

f. Todos los días

g. En avión

h. Hacer buceo

i. Salir al centro

3. Spot and correct the grammar and spelling mistakes note: in several cases a word is missing

a. Voy hacer deporte

b. Voy a paso una semana alí

c. Voy a quedarme un hotel lujo

d. Vamos quedarno en una hotel

e. Me gustaria jugar un fútbol

f. Vamos a sallir al centero

g. Voy a voy a la playa

h. Voy a jugar a mes amigos

4. Categories: Positive or Negative?
Write P or N

a. Será divertido: ___**P**___

b. Será aburrido: _____

c. Será agradable: _____

d. Será relajante: _____

e. Será interesante: _____

f. Será terrible: _____

g. Será curioso: _____

h. Será asqueroso: _____

i. Será fascinante: _____

j. Será impresionante: _____

5. Translate into Spanish

a. I am going to rest

b. I am going to go diving

c. We are going to go to the beach

d. I am going to sunbathe

e. I would like to go sightseeing

f. I am going to stay in…

g. …a cheap hotel

h. We are going to spend 2 weeks

i. I am going to go by plane

j. It will be fun

Revision Quickie 6: Daily Routine/House/Home life/Holidays

1. Match-up

En las afueras	In the garden
En el cuarto de baño	In the living room
En la cocina	In my bedroom
En mi casa	In my house
En el jardín	In the shower
En mi habitación	In the dining room
En el comedor	In the bathroom
En la ducha	In the kitchen
En el salón	On the outskirts

2. Complete with the missing letters

a. Me du_____   *I shower*

b. Me le_____   *I get up*

c. Ve___ la tele   *I watch television*

d. Le___ tebeos   *I read comics*

e. Sa___ de casa   *I leave home*

f. Ll____ al colegio   *I arrive at school*

g. Co___ el autobús   *I catch the bus*

h. Me vi_____   *I get dressed*

i De_____   *I have breakfast*

3. Spot and correct any of the sentences below which do not make sense

a. Me ducho en el frigorífico

b. Como en la ducha

c. Preparo la comida en mi dormitorio

d. Me lavo el pelo en el salón

e. Voy a mi dormitorio en autobús

f. Juego al ping-pong con mi perro

g. El sofá está en la cocina

h. Veo la tele en el horno

i. Duermo en el armario

j. Pongo el coche en mi dormitorio

4. Split sentences

Veo	el autobús
Escucho	cereales
Leo	la tele
Cojo	un café
Desayuno	música
Voy a ir a Japón	tebeos
Bebo	deberes
Subo fotos	en avión
Hago mis	a Instagram
Arreglo	a las cartas
Trabajo en	mi dormitorio
Juego	el ordenador

5. Match the opposites

Bueno	Malsano
Simpático	Malo
Fácil	Hermoso
Divertido	Antipático
Sano	Difícil
Feo	Aburrido
Caro	Rápido
Lento	Alto
A menudo	Barato
Nunca	Raramente
Bajo	Siempre

 **THE LANGUAGE GYM**

6. Complete with the missing words

a. Voy a ir a Japón _____ avión

b. Voy a ir a Italia _____ mis padres

c. Nunca juego _____ fútbol

d. Odio _____ cricket

e. Me quedo en un hotel _____ lujo

f. Voy al parque una vez _____ semana

g. Me meto ____ Internet

h. Subo fotos ____ Instagram

7. Draw a line in between each word

a. Megustamuchojugaralbaloncesto

b. Veolateleyescuchomúsica

c. Enmitiempolibrejuegoalosvideojuegos

d. VoyairaAlemaniaencoche

e. Voyaquedarmeenunhoteldelujo

f. Porlamañanavoyairalaplaya

g. Voyairdemarchaestesábado

h. Nuncahagomisdeberes

8. Spot the translation mistakes and correct them

a. Me levanto temprano: *I go to bed early*

b. Odio el baloncesto: *I hate volleyball*

c. Voy a ir a la piscina: *I am going to go to the beach*

d. No vamos a hacer nada: *I am not going to do anything*

e. Voy a nadar: *I am going to run*

f. Voy a viajar en coche: *I am going to travel by plane*

g. Voy a quedarme en un hotel de lujo:

I am going to stay in a cheap hotel

h. Voy a ver una película: *I am going to watch a series*

9. Translate into English:

a. Cojo el avión

b. Voy a ir

c. Voy a quedarme

d. Me lavo

e. Veo una película

f. Arreglo mi dormitorio

g. Ceno verduras

h. Desayuno huevos

i. No hago nada

j. Trabajo en el ordenador

10. Translate into Spanish

a. I shower then I have breakfast

b. Tomorrow I am going to go to Japan

c. I tidy up my room every day

d. I never play basketball

e. I get up early

f. I eat a lot for breakfast

g. I am going to go to Italy by car

h. In my free time I play chess and read books

i. I spend many hours on the Internet

11. Translate into Spanish

a. I have dinner: C_ _ _ _

b. I watch: V_ _

c. I do: H_ _ _

d. I clean: L_ _ _ _ _ _

e. I read: L_ _

f. I work: T_ _ _ _ _ _ _

g. I rest: D_ _ _ _ _ _ _ _

h. I tidy up: A_ _ _ _ _ _ _

i. I catch: C_ _ _

THE LANGUAGE GYM

Question Skills 4: Daily routine/House/Home life/Holidays

1. Complete the questions with the correct option

a. ¿_____hora te levantas?

b. ¿_____ pasas tu tiempo libre?

c. ¿_____haces después del colegio?

d. ¿_____horas pasas en el ordenador?

e. ¿_____ juegas a la Play?

f. ¿_____ no haces más deporte?

g. ¿_____ vas el viernes por la noche?

h. ¿_____ es tu habitación preferida?

Adónde	A qué	Cuántas	Qué
Por qué	Cuál	Cómo	Con quién

3. Match each statement below to one of the questions included in activity 1 above

a. Dos o tres

b. Lo paso jugando en el ordenador

c. Con mi hermano menor

d. A eso de las seis

e. Voy a discotecas con mi mejor amigo

f. Vuelvo a casa

g. Porque soy perezoso y no tengo tiempo

h. Mi dormitorio, por supuesto

5. Translate

a. Where is your room?

b. Where do you go after school?

c. What do you do in your free time?

d. Until what time do you study?

e. How long do you spend on the Internet?

f. What is your favourite pastime?

g. What do you do to help in the house?

2. Split questions

¿A qué	no juegas al fútbol con nosotros?
¿Qué comes	veces a la semana vas al gimnasio?
¿Qué	hora vuelves a casa?
¿Con	haces footing?
¿Por qué	para el desayuno?
¿Cuántas	quién juegas al ajedrez?
¿Dónde	haces en tu tiempo libre?
¿Cómo pasas	tus padres en casa?
¿Ayudas a	tu tiempo libre?

4. Translate into Spanish

a. Who?

b. When?

c. Who with?

d. Why?

e. How many? (feminine plural)

f. How much? (masculine singular)

g. Which ones?

h. Where to?

i. Do you do...?

j. Can you...?

k. Where is...?

l. How many hours?

m. How many people?

VOCABULARY TESTS

On the following pages you will find one vocabulary test for every unit in the book. You could set them as class assessments or as homeworks at the end of a unit. Students could also use them to practice independently.

1a. Translate the following sentences (worth one point each) into Spanish

What is your name?	
My name is Pablo	
How old are you?	
I am five years old	
I am seven years old	
I am nine years old	
I am ten years old	
I am eleven years old	
I am twelve years old	
I am thirteen years old	
Score	**/10**

1b. Translate the following sentences (worth two points each) into Spanish

What is your brother called?	
What is your sister called?	
My brother is called Mario	
My sister is fourteen years old	
My brother is fifteen years old	
I don't have any siblings	
My name is Jean and I am French	
I have a brother who is called Felipe	
I live in the capital of Japan	
I live in the capital of France	
Score	**/20**

1a. Translate the following sentences (worth one point each) into Spanish

My name is Sergio	
I am eleven years old	
I am fifteen years old	
I am eighteen years old	
The 3rd May	
The 4th April	
The 5th June	
The 6th September	
The 10th October	
The 8th July	
Score	**/10**

1b. Translate the following sentences (worth two points each) into Spanish

I am 17. My birthday is on 21st June	
My brother is called Julio. He is 19	
My sister is called Maria. She is 22	
My brother's birthday is on 23rd March	
My name is Felipe. I am 15. My birthday is on 27th July	
My name is Gregorio. I am 18. My birthday is on 30th June	
When is your birthday?	
Is your birthday in October or November?	
My brother is called Pedro. His birthday is on 31st January	
Is your birthday in May or June?	
Score	**/20**

1a. Translate the following sentences (worth one point each) into Spanish

Black hair	
Dark brown (black) eyes	
Blonde hair	
Blue eyes	
My name is Gabriela	
I am 12 years old	
I have long hair	
I have short hair	
I have green eyes	
I have brown eyes	
Score	**/10**

1b. Translate the following sentences (worth two points each) into Spanish

I have grey hair and grey eyes	
I have red straight hair	
I have curly white hair	
I have brown hair and brown eyes	
I wear glasses and have spikey hair	
I don't wear glasses and I have a beard	
My brother has blond hair and has a moustache	
My brother is 22 years old and has a crew cut	
Do you wear glasses?	
My sister has blue eyes and wavy black hair	
Score	**/20**

1a. Translate the following sentences (worth one point each) into Spanish

My name is	
I am from	
I live in	
In a house	
In a modern building	
In an old building	
On the outskirts	
In the centre	
On the coast	
In Zaragoza	
Score	**/10**

1b. Translate the following sentences (worth two points each) into Spanish

My brother is called Paco	
My sister is called Alejandra	
I live in an old building	
I live in a modern building	
I live in a beautiful house on the coast	
I live in an ugly house in the centre	
I am from Madrid but live in the centre of Buenos Aires	
I am 15 years old and I am Spanish	
I am Spanish, from Zaragoza but I live in Bogota, in Colombia	
I live in a small apartment in the countryside	
Score	**/20**

1a. Translate the following sentences (worth one point each) into Spanish

My younger brother	
My older brother	
My older sister	
My younger sister	
My father	
My mother	
My uncle	
My auntie	
My male cousin	
My female cousin	
Score	**/10**

1b. Translate the following sentences (worth two points each) into Spanish

In my family there are four people	
My father, my mother and two brothers	
I don't get along with my older brother	
My older sister is 22	
My younger sister is 16	
My grandfather is 78	
My grandmother is 67	
My uncle is 54	
My auntie is 44	
My female cousin is 17	
Score	**/20**

1a. Translate the following sentences (worth one point each) into Spanish

Tall (masculine)	
Short (feminine)	
Ugly (masculine)	
Good-looking (masculine)	
Generous (masculine)	
Boring (feminine)	
Intelligent (masculine)	
Muscular (masculine)	
Good (feminine)	
Fat (masculine)	
Score	**/10**

1b. Translate the following sentences (worth two points each) into Spanish

My mother is strict and boring	
My father is stubborn and unfriendly	
My older sister is intelligent and hard-working	
My younger sister is sporty	
In my family I have five people	
I get along with my older sister because she is nice	
I don't get along with my younger sister because she is annoying	
I love my grandparents because they are funny and generous	
What are your parents like?	
My uncle and auntie are fifty and I don't get along with them	
Score	**/20**

1a. Translate the following sentences (worth one point each) into Spanish

A horse	
A rabbit	
A dog	
A turtle	
A bird	
A parrot	
A duck	
A guinea pig	
A cat	
A mouse	
Score	**/10**

1b. Translate the following sentences (worth three points each) into Spanish

I have a white horse	
I have a green turtle	
At home we have two fish	
My sister has a spider	
I don't have pets	
My friend Pedro has a blue bird	
My cat is very fat	
I have a snake that is called Adam	
My duck is funny and noisy	
How many pets do you have at home?	
Score	**/30**

1a. Translate the following sentences (worth one point each) into Spanish

He is a cook	
He is a journalist	
She is a waitress	
She is a nurse	
He is a househusband	
She is a doctor	
He is a teacher	
She is a businesswoman	
He is a hairdresser	
She is a farmer	
Score	**/10**

1b. Translate the following sentences (worth three points each) into Spanish

My uncle is a cook	
My mother is a nurse	
My grandparents don't work	
My sister works as a teacher	
My auntie is an actress	
My (male) cousin is a student	
My (male) cousins are lawyers	
He doesn't like it because it is hard	
He likes it because it is gratifying	
He hates it because it is stressful	
Score	**/30**

 **THE LANGUAGE GYM**

1a. Translate the following sentences (worth two points each) into Spanish

He is taller than me	
He is more generous than her	
She is less fat than him	
He is slimmer than her	
She is better looking than him	
She is more talkative than me	
I am more funny than him	
My dog is less noisy	
My rabbit is more fun	
She is as talkative as me	
Score	/20

1b. Translate the following sentences (worth 3 points each) into Spanish

My brother is stronger than me	
My mother is shorter than my father	
My uncle is better looking than my father	
My older sister is more talkative than my younger sister	
My sister and I are taller than my cousins	
My grandfather is less strict than my grandmother	
My friend Paco is friendlier than my friend Felipe	
My rabbit is quieter than my duck	
My cat is fatter than my dog	
My mouse is faster than my turtle	
Score	/30

1a. Translate the following sentences (worth one point each) into Spanish

I have a pen	
I have a ruler	
I have a rubber	
In my bag	
In my pencil case	
My friend Paco	
Pedro has	
I don't have	
A purple exercise book	
A yellow pencil sharpener	
Score	**/10**

1b. Translate the following sentences (worth three points each) into Spanish

In my schoolbag I have four books	
I have a yellow pencil case	
I have a red schoolbag	
I don't have black markers	
There are two blue pens	
My friend Paco has a pencil sharpener	
Do you guys have a rubber?	
Do you have a red pen?	
Is there a ruler in your pencil case?	
What is there in your schoolbag?	
Score	**/30**

1a. Translate the following sentences (worth three points each) into Spanish

I don't like milk	
I love meat	
I don't like fish much	
I hate chicken	
Fruit is good	
Honey is healthy	
I prefer mineral water	
Milk is disgusting	
Chocolate is delicious	
Cheese is unhealthy	
Score	**/30**

1b. Translate the following sentences (worth five points each) into Spanish

I love chocolate because it is delicious	
I like apples a lot because they are healthy	
I don't like red meat because it is unhealthy	
I don't like sausages because they are unhealthy	
I love fish with potatoes	
I hate seafood because it is disgusting	
I like fruit because it is light and delicious	
I like spicy chicken with vegetables	
I like eggs because they are rich in protein	
Roast chicken is tastier than fried fish	
Score	**/50**

1a. Translate the following sentences (worth one point each) into Spanish

I have breakfast	
I have lunch	
I have afternoon 'snack'	
I have dinner	
It is delicious	
It is light	
It is disgusting	
It is refreshing	
It is healthy	
It is sweet	
Score	**/10**

1b. Translate the following sentences (worth three points each) into Spanish

I eat eggs and coffee for breakfast	
I have seafood for lunch	
I never have dinner	
For snack I have two 'toasts'	
In the morning I usually eat fruit	
I love meat because it is tasty	
From time to time I eat cheese	
In the evening I eat little	
We eat a lot of meat and fish	
I don't eat sweets often	
Score	**/30**

1a. Translate the following sentences (worth two points each) into Spanish

A red skirt	
A blue suit	
A green scarf	
Black trousers	
A white shirt	
A brown hat	
A yellow T-shirt	
Blue jeans	
A purple tie	
Grey shoes	
Score	**/20**

1b. Translate the following sentences (worth three points each) into Spanish

I often wear a black baseball cap	
At home I wear a blue track suit	
At school we wear a green uniform	
At the beach I wear a red bathing suit	
My sister always wears jeans	
My brother never wears a watch	
My mother wears branded clothes	
I very rarely wear suits	
My girlfriend wears a pretty dress	
My brothers always wears trainers	
Score	**/30**

THE LANGUAGE GYM

1a. Translate the following sentences (worth two points each) into Spanish

I do my homework	
I play football	
I go rock climbing	
I go cycling	
I do weights	
I go to the swimming pool	
I do sport	
I go horse riding	
I play tennis	
I go to the beach	
Score	/20

1b. Translate the following sentences (worth five points each) into Spanish

I never play basketball because it is boring	
I play PlayStation with my friends	
My father and I go fishing from time to time	
My brother and I go to the gym every day	
I do weights and go jogging every day	
When the weather is nice, we go hiking	
When the weather is bad, I play chess	
My father goes swimming at the weekend	
My younger brothers go to the park after school	
In my free time, I go rock climbing or to my friend's house	
Score	/50

1a. Translate the following sentences (worth two points each) into Spanish

When the weather is nice	
When the weather is bad	
When it is sunny	
When it is cold	
When it is hot	
I go skiing	
I play with my friends	
I go to the mall	
I go to the gym	
I go on a bike ride	
Score	**/20**

1b. Translate the following sentences (worth four points each) into Spanish

When the weather is nice, I go jogging	
When it rains, we go to the sports centre and do weights	
At the weekend, I do my homework and a bit of sport	
When it is hot, she goes to the beach or goes cycling	
When I have time, I go jogging with my father	
When there are storms, we stay at home and play cards	
When it is sunny and the sky is clear, they go to the park	
On Fridays and Saturdays, I go clubbing with my girlfriend	
We never do sport. We play on the computer or on PlayStation	
When it snows, we go to the mountain and ski	
Score	**/40**

1a. Translate the following sentences (worth one point each) into Spanish

I get up	
I have breakfast	
I eat	
I drink	
I go to bed	
Around six o' clock	
I rest	
At noon	
At midnight	
I do my homework	
Score	/10

1b. Translate the following sentences (worth three points each) into Spanish

Around 7.00 in the morning I have breakfast	
I shower then I get dressed	
I eat then I brush my teeth	
Around 8 o'clock in the evening I have dinner	
I go to school by bus	
I watch television in my room	
I go back home at 4.30	
From 6 to 7 I play on the computer	
Afterwards, around 11.30, I go to bed	
My daily routine is simple	
Score	/30

 **THE LANGUAGE GYM**

1a. Translate the following sentences (worth one point each) into Spanish

I live	
In a new house	
In an old house	
In a small house	
In a big house	
On the coast	
In the mountains	
In an ugly apartment	
On the outskirts	
In the centre of town	
Score	**/10**

1b. Translate the following sentences (worth three points each) into Spanish

In my house there are four rooms	
My favourite room is the kitchen	
I enjoy relaxing in the living room	
In my apartment there are seven rooms	
My parents live in a big house	
My uncle lives in a small house	
We live near the coast	
My friend Paco lives on a farm	
My cousins live in Barcelona	
My parents and I live in a cosy house	
Score	**/30**

1a. Translate the following sentences (worth one point each) into Spanish

I chat with my mother	
I play on the PlayStation	
I read magazines	
I read comics	
I watch films	
I listen to music	
I rest	
I do my homework	
I go on a bike ride	
I leave the house	
Score	**/10**

1b. Translate the following sentences (worth three points each) into Spanish

I never tidy up my room	
I rarely help my parents	
I brush my teeth three times a week	
I upload many photos onto Instagram	
Every day I watch series on Netflix	
I have breakfast at around 7.30	
After school I rest in the garden	
When I have time, I play with my brother	
I usually leave home at 8 o'clock	
From time to time I watch a movie	
Score	**/30**

1a. Translate the following sentences (worth two points each) into Spanish

I am going to go	
I am going to stay	
I am going to play	
I am going to eat	
I am going to drink	
I am going to rest	
I am going to go sightseeing	
I am going to go to the beach	
I am going to do sport	
I am going to dance	
Score	/20

1b. Translate the following sentences (worth five points each) into Spanish

We are going to buy souvenirs and clothes	
I am going to stay in a cheap hotel near the beach	
We are going to stay there for three weeks	
I am going to spend two weeks there with my family	
We are going to go on holiday to Argentina tomorrow	
We are going to Spain for two weeks and we are going to travel by plane	
I would like to do sport, go to the beach and dance	
We are going to spend 3 weeks in Italy and we are going to stay in a campsite	
We are going to go stay in a luxury hotel near the beach	
We are going to go sightseeing and shopping every day	
Score	/50

The End

We hope you have enjoyed using this workbook and found it useful!

As many of you will appreciate, the penguin is a fantastic animal. At Language Gym, we hold it as a symbol of resilience, bravery and good humour; able to thrive in the harshest possible environments, and with, arguably the best gait in the animal kingdom (black panther or penguin, you choose). In Spanish, it is also the best example of the ü (dieresis); this is a symbol that helps distinguish "gui" (pronounced like the 'gi' in English "gift) and "güi"(pronounced like the 'gui' in "penguin"). The same occurs with 'gue' (ge) and 'güe' (gue).

There are several hidden penguins (pictures)in this book, did you spot them all?

Printed in Great Britain
by Amazon

86407961R00113